IF YOUR cat COULD TALK...

IF YOUR cat COULD TALK...

Based on material from *Know Your Cat*

DR BRUCE FOGLE

LONDON, NEW YORK, MELBOURNE,
MUNICH, AND DELHI

Editor Miezan van Zyl
Managing Editor Sarah Larter
Senior Managing Art Editor Philip Ormerod
DTP Designers Laragh Kedwell, Rob Strachan
Production Controller Tony Phipps
Picture Librarian Claire Bowers
Publisher Jonathan Metcalf
Art Director Bryn Walls
US Editor Christine Heilman

PRODUCED BY
SANDS PUBLISHING SOLUTIONS
Project Editors David & Sylvia Tombesi-Walton
Project Art Editor Simon Murrell

First published in Great Britain in 1992 as
Know Your Cat by Dorling Kindersley Limited.
This fully revised edition published in
the United States in 2007 by
DK Publishing
375 Hudson Street
New York, New York 10014

07 08 09 10 11   10 9 8 7 6 5 4 3 2 1

ID066 – August 2007

ISBN: 978-0-7566-2643-3

DK books are available at special discounts when purchased in bulk
for sales promotions, premiums, fund-raising, or educational use.
For details, contact: DK Publishing Special Markets, 375 Hudson
Street, New York, New York 10014 or SpecialSales@dk.com.

Reproduced in Singapore by Colourscan
Printed and bound in China by Sheck Wah Tong

Discover more at
www.dk.com

Contents

Foreword

There was a time when I saw cats at my veterinary clinic only to inoculate and neuter them when they were young or to assist their dying when they were old. It seems hard to imagine now, but until very recently—so recently that I was already a practicing veterinarian—cats had little intrinsic value for many people. I mean emotional value. Social or psychological value. Until the second half of the 20th century, the decades when cats moved permanently into our homes—onto our sofas, onto our beds, under the covers, into our hearts—the cat's values to us were practical. This was a utilitarian species: cats caught mice.

The domestic cat's natural independence was seen as much as aloofness as anything else. Getting ill or injured or dying was, thought many, part of the reality of marching to your own drum. Dogs were dependent and needed us. Cats took care of themselves. One consequence of our attitude toward them was that, of all the species we live with, we understood the cat the least.

Oh, what a change! Where cats once constituted less than 10 percent of the pets I saw at my clinic, today they are in the majority. Where once only farmers and "cataholics" kept cats, today they are in all types of households, especially in homes with a history of dog-keeping and little knowledge of feline behavior. That can be problematic, because some people expect their cats to behave like dogs that meow.

Here's one of the most typical scenarios that takes place at the veterinary clinic. An apartment-dwelling cat owner calls. She and her husband both work, and feeling sorry for their cat, who is left at home alone each day, they acquired a new kitten as a playmate for their feline friend. Now their cat is: (a) urinating outside the litter box; (b) pooping by the door; (c) hissing at, spitting at, or beating up the new arrival; (d) withdrawing its affection from its human owners; or (e) placing an ad in the local newspaper seeking a new home. "What can we do?" an anxious and concerned voice asks.

Cats are not sensuous, silent dogs, with crampons for climbing. Their social needs are considerably different from those of dogs, or of us, for that matter. More

than any other domesticated species, they are content with themselves. Cats have an enviably refined sense of self. They know exactly who they are and what they need and want. In human terms, that can be interpreted as imperiousness or aloofness, which is why the saying "Dogs believe they are human; cats believe they are God" brings nods of acknowledgment from so many cat owners. The equally appreciated variation has it that "Dogs have owners; cats have staff." So true.

As our relationship with cats intensified during the 20th century, naturalists began to look at their behavior more seriously, and in the 1970s and 80s, countless observational studies of domestic cats, both in home and outdoor environments, were published in ethology journals. Now their behavior was more accurately understood. Here was a matriarchal species with the potential to be much more sociable than was once thought. It all depended upon early learning, when the kitten was less than 50 days old.

To me, what is so alluring about the cat is its natural sensuousness. More than with any other domesticated species, living with a cat provides us with a window on the natural world. Cat watching is addictive. I promise you, it's as satisfying as a daily natural-history program on TV. (No wonder so many of the orange tabbies I see are named Tiger.) Cats are honest with their feelings, but we still misinterpret some of them. For example, people familiar with dogs can misinterpret a cat's wagging tail as a happy signal. Equally, cats can, and should, be trained to come when called, but they don't respond to all the methods of training that dogs respond to. Their needs are different from those of dogs because they evolved to fill a different role in nature. *If Your Cat Could Talk…* introduces you to the idiosyncrasies of how cats think and why cats do what they do. Knowing that guarantees that living with a cat is more rewarding and fulfilling for you but, just as important, for your cat too.

DR. BRUCE FOGLE

Introduction

Cats are self-sufficient, self-possessed, independent, powerful, sensuous in motion, and quiet in movement. The domestic cat is a magnificent animal, exceptionally well designed, more agile than dogs or any other domestic animal, with parts that wear out only with old age. As beautiful and alluring as cats are, we frequently misunderstand them, because, unlike dogs, cats are in many ways quite different from us. I wonder whether we really would like to know what cats would say if they could talk. Those of us who live with them know that as well as their uttering—or muttering—some mumbled words of affection, there would be an equal number of fiercer expletives coming from their mouths. We know, too, that they would use only a few words to express themselves, for cats control their emotions far better than we do. Dogs might be prone to florid adjectives; cats would talk in simpler terms.

A RECENT RELATIONSHIP

Dogs, like humans, are sociable pack animals. Both species evolved to have a reliance upon, and enjoyment of, the companionship of their own kind. In the process of doing so, a dynamic range of welcoming, or "come closer," body-language signals developed: we smile and wave; dogs look alert, drop their ears back, and wag their tails. But cats come from a different beginning. They evolved—or, to be more accurate, they are in the process of evolving—from solitary hunters to a more sociable species. They moved into human society only 5,000 years ago, later than any other domesticated animal. Their numbers remained strong but steady until, quite suddenly, during the latter part of the last century, they became our most popular pets. In North America there are now more than 80 million, in the European Union another 80 million. They are

Beautiful but misunderstood
Throughout time, cats have received a lot of "bad press." Fortunately, we are now beginning to see a change in this perception.

Early social contact
In order to bring out the best in cats as a domestic pet, it is essential that they are socialized early in their lives, both with humans and with any other species of animal.

more popular than dogs in most developed countries. With millions more pet cats in Africa, Asia, Central and South America, Australasia, and on various islands worldwide, there are more than 200 million domestic cats living with people and an equal number living by their own wits—overwhelmingly the most successful feline that has ever existed.

Domestic cats are divided into two main groups: domestic pet cats and feral cats. Domestic pet cats live with human company. Usually raised by us, they are content to live in our homes and share our food and affection. Curiously, for cats, humans are less threatening than other cats. We often make better companions for them than other cats do.

Feral cats are domestic cats born in the wild and raised outside human contact. There are no genetic differences between feral and pet cats. The only

difference is in their early upbringing. If they are denied routine human contact during the important first seven weeks of life, they will always retain a fear of us. Repeated early contact with humans is vital for a cat to develop a strong physical and emotional relationship with people.

EVOLVING BEHAVIOR

The North African wild cat, from which our pets evolved, was a hunter. Even today, domestic cats retain a powerfully unmitigated urge to hunt. However, when North African cats chose to move into human communities—and it was their choice—they changed from solitary hunters and became scavengers and beggars, too. In the wild, kittens grow out of playing with each other when the more serious concerns of hunting for food, protecting themselves, and finding mates become dominant imperatives in their lives. Pet cats, with their daily needs of food, safety, security, and warmth taken care of, have no need to "grow up," so

Hunter scavenger
Despite their domestication, cats are still perfectly able to return to their roots as expert hunters. Indeed, they will kill rodents and birds even if they do not need a meal.

Breed differences
It is not just the look of cats that may be changed through selective breeding; their personalities can be altered, too.

they often remain playful when mature, perpetual kittens dependent upon their human family for their physical and emotional well-being.

More new breeds of cat are being created now than ever before—more than 25 breeds in the past 25 years. Each new breed has obvious physical attributes such as the length, texture, and color of the coat, but there are additional differences between breeds. Feline behavior changes with age, but through selective breeding, some breeds are noisier than others, or less clean, or friendlier with other household pets. Some breeds live longer than others. Now that so many of us live in such intimacy with our cats, we intervene in their breeding not just to perpetuate desired physical characteristics, but also to emphasize specific temperaments and characters.

A clean animal
One might be forgiven for thinking that when a cat is not sleeping, it is washing itself. Cats have a very strong sense of personal hygiene.

INTERPRETING CAT BEHAVIOR

It is easy to misunderstand what cats mean when they do what they do, to misinterpret their actions, to forget that their reasons for doing things can be different from ours. We are proud of our cats and laud their intelligence when we train them so easily to use litter boxes, and we are upset with them when they scratch our furniture. Yet both of these activities—the need to use a dedicated toilet site and the need to mark territory—are equally normal and natural to a cat. It is easy to confuse how we want our cats to behave and how cats want to behave. To understand how cats behave, it is vital to remember that, although their brains are made up of the same components as ours, they have different or varying forms of "intelligence" from us, some of which are better developed than ours and some less developed. For example, their understanding of personal hygiene, a concept of intelligence called "intrapersonal" by academics, is highly developed. Cats routinely, ritually cleanse themselves and keep their resting places clean and odor-free. Their "spatial" intelligence, their ability to mentally map comparatively large territories, has diminished with domestication, and this alone may account for the fact that the domesticated cat's brain weighs less than its North African wild cat ancestor's. On the other hand, their "kinesthetic" intelligence, their knowledge of motion and forces, is superior to ours. Watch a cat prepare to leap up, and you see that its capacity to use exactly the right amount of power to neither overshoot nor undershoot the landing target is just magnificent, undiminished by domestication.

THE THINKING CAT

Do cats really think? Of course they do. After all, look at your cat's reaction when it sees you readying the cat carrier for a visit to the vet. Do cats have emotions? The answer is a resounding yes. And it is not anthropomorphic to credit cats with emotions such as jealousy, for both humans and cats have identical neurochemicals and regions in the brain responsible for emotion. If cats could talk, exactly what would they say? Throughout this book, I am going to put words in the cat's mouth. Most of these are fantasy thoughts—what we would like to think our cats would say if they could talk. I am doing so, in part in jest and in part seriously, to act as a reminder that they do have feelings and emotions, although I am aware that I am being generous in reading their thoughts in this way. In truth, selfishness is a more powerful motor of behavior and emotion in cats than it is in dogs or in us.

Every day, on the examining table at my veterinary clinic, cats are telling me something. In many instances, what they are saying would probably not be suitable for publication, but my point is that through their body language, their activities, and their demeanor, cats are skilled communicators. I hope this book helps interpret what they are saying.

Telling it like it is
Cats are incredibly adept at making their feelings known. A swish of the tail, a squeak of the voice, a swipe of the paw: each gets a message across.

1 WHAT IS A CAT?

The domestic cat is a seducer. In the shortest of time, it has evolved from a small, relatively insignificant North African carnivore into our most populous animal companion. Throughout Europe and North America, owned cats now outnumber owned dogs, and in many regions there are as many unowned domestic cats, feral individuals, surviving on their wits, usually with a little help from their human friends.

Genetic studies confirm that all breeds of cats are descended from the North African wild cat. Contrary to what was once postulated, neither the European wild cat nor the North African jungle cat participated in the domestic cat's development.

This sensuous, aesthetically appealing species is "self-domesticated": its ancestors made the decision to live with our ancestors, and this happened just 5,000 years ago—a fraction of a second in evolutionary terms. The change necessary for domestication—a reduced fear of humans—came from within, and it is possible that this modification of the "fight or flight" impulse spontaneously occurred within a single line of African wild cats. The success of that modification led to their descendants successfully inhabiting human settlements, particularly the grain stores of Egypt—an ideal hunting ground for small rodents.

The cat's ability to protect stored food from rodents, and homes from poisonous snakes, together with its natural beauty, its often mysterious behavior, and its high fertility, led to the cat's being venerated in Egypt.

Variations on a theme
Within the North African wild cat's genes was the potential for all the coats and colors seen in cats today, such as in this selection of classic Persian, orange tom, colorpoint Persian and Siamese cats.

What was prized in that country was coveted elsewhere, and through trade, migration, and conquest, the domesticated North African wild cat—now the "domestic cat"—was transported around the Mediterranean and eventually throughout Europe and Asia, always revered for its practical and utilitarian value. Cats were self-sufficient, feeding and cleaning themselves, while also efficient rodent killers. In Europe, after the Crusades, cats were for a time associated with Islam, and this evolved into their being equated with witchcraft and devilry. Cats, and often their owners, were persecuted. Even today, vestiges of that hostility remain, as in the use of a cat as a Halloween symbol.

The modern domestic cat has overcome these prejudices. It accompanied the first Europeans to the Americas, southern Africa, and Australasia, and in all these regions—even on isolated, often environmentally hostile islands—it adapted, survived, and thrived. Today, domestic cats inhabit all continents except Antarctica and all the major islands of the world.

Selective breeding for amenable personalities, coupled with the cat's natural ability to adapt, means the species has become, in effect, forever caught in the hinterland of adolescence. The modern cat is "forever young," raised to depend on us for its food and protection. In the last 100 years it has moved out of the barn into our backyards, then into our homes and our hearts. It is dependent and independent, content to live with us, to adapt to our culture, but ever capable, when necessary, of "growing up" and reverting back to nature.

Meet the ancestors

ALL MODERN carnivorous mammal species, including the cat, evolved from a single family of early mammals called the miacids, which thrived in the post-dinosaur age around 60 million years ago. It is thought that the secret to the miacids' success and longevity over other carnivores was their bigger brain, enabling them to adapt to change. These long-bodied, short-legged mammals evolved into the carnivore families we know today. From these early mammals the first "cat" developed—*Proailurus*, a half-cat, half-civet carnivore.

The successor to *Proailurus* was *Pseudaelurus*, which arrived 20 million years ago, walked on the tips of its toes, and had stabbing canine teeth. These two species are the first members of the modern cat family, *Felidae*, within which there are eight major lineages. The first line to emerge included panthers; later lines produced smaller animals such as the bay cat, ocelot, and, 6.2 million years ago, the domestic cat's immediate ancestor, the now-extinct *Felis lunensis*—the ancestor of all small wild cats in Europe, Africa, and Asia today.

Cranium

Mandible

Fossil evidence?
The oldest tiger fossils have been found in China, but early big cats spread around the world, with lions heading as far west as North America and as far north as Siberia. Leopards and jaguars dispersed through Europe, Asia, Africa, and the Americas.

Giving it a name

Although the word "tabby" is thought to derive from *atabi*, a striped cloth pattern woven by silk weavers in the Attabiah region near Baghdad, Iraq, and "puss" from Pasht or Bast, the name of the Egyptian cat-headed goddess, the origin of the word "cat" is uncertain. The Latin word *cattus* was first used in Europe in the 4th century and is the origin of the English "cat," German *Katze*, Scandinavian *kat* or *katt*, French *chat*, Italian *gatto*, Spanish and Portuguese *gato*, and Slavic *kot*, *kotka*, and *kochka*. It is thought that the Latin word may have been derived from the Arabic *quttah* or Egyptian Coptic *chau*.

Non-cat regions
Despite the cat's best efforts, some parts of the world were feline-free until man carried the domestic cat along trade routes. In Australia, separated from the rest of the world around 85 million years before the evolution of the cat, a marsupial carnivore called the tiger quoll, *Dasyurus maculatus* (left), fulfilled the small predator role. North America was free from small cats, with the predator's niche being filled by the *Mustelidae* family, which includes minks and skunks.

Carnivore ancestors

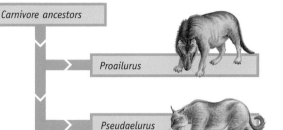

Proailurus

Pseudaelurus

Panthera → Panthera leo

Lions are known to have existed for more than 3 million years

Felis

Felis lunensis

Felis silvestris catus

Cat evolution

Experts disagree on the exact details of feline evolution, but fossil evidence suggests that there is a direct relationship between ancient "catlike," forest-dwelling carnivores and later "catlike" species such as *Proailurus* and *Pseudaelurus*. The *Panthera* evolutionary line, leading to present-day lions and panthers, evolved around 10.8 million years ago, while animals in the cat's own genus, *Felis*, emerged 6.2 million years ago.

The domestic cat

Biologists have long questioned whether the domestic cat (*Felis silvestris catus*) descends wholly from the African wild cat (*Felis silvestris lybica*) or whether the European wild cat (*Felis silvestris europeus*) also played a part. Recent DNA studies in Italy of all three cat types showed that the domestic cat descends wholly from the African wild cat.

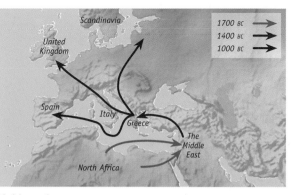

Scandinavia	
United Kingdom	1700 BC →
	1400 BC →
	1000 BC →
Spain Italy Greece	
	The Middle East
North Africa	

Divide and conquer

Phoenician traders were the first to transport large numbers of domesticated felines out of Africa. Cats appeared in what is now Israel and Palestine more than 3,700 years ago, and in Greece a few hundred years later. By 3,000 years ago, they had spread across the Mediterranean region.

The cat evolves

YOUR PET CAT, a descendant of the North African wild cat, retains instincts and behaviors similar to those of his wild cousins. The wild cat is highly adaptable, capable of responding to novel situations, and shows little fear of humans. In fact, its natural behavioral makeup includes an ability to live in close proximity to people. Thousands of years ago, the wild cat chose of its own accord to become domesticated, willingly relinquishing the life of the lone hunter. The short-haired coat of the North African wild cat consists of two types of hair: short, fine down hairs and longer, thicker guard hairs. Most long-haired cats evolved as the result of a genetic mutation that allowed the down hair to continue to grow. The long down hairs tangle easily. The long-haired Norwegian forest cat and the Maine coon have longer guard hairs that do not get matted, so these cats are able to survive without help from us with grooming.

Living close to man
Forebear of today's domestic cat, the North African wild cat is drawn to human settlements, where it can scavenge for a meal.

"Yes,
I'm woolly
and wild."

Long guard hairs

Woolly undercoat

Instinctive hunter
Even as the North African wild cat evolved into a domestic animal, it retained the ability to be self-sufficient. The Norwegian forest cat, a descendant of the tamed African wild cat, returned to the wild, where it survived as a superb hunter.

"Wild? Me? Let me count the ways."

Head is small in relation to large body

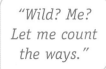

"I mean, really, what's not to love?"

Thick coat helps survival in cold weather

Surviving alone
Timid and reclusive, the European wild cat does not have the genetic potential to alter its behavior, and so has not been able to adapt to living with man. Impossible to tame, this cat has had no part in the evolution of the pet cat.

Maine coon
My family cat Milly, a Maine coon descended from hardy American farm cats, has a luxurious coat to cope with a harsh climate. Thanks to her large size, she can catch rabbits, the most widely available prey.

Thick bushy tail

Becoming domesticated

CHOOSING TO LIVE near human settlements, the North African wild cat gradually shifted from hunting for his food in the wild to scavenging. Villages provided a source of food, and the cat's diet was supplemented with the mice and rats that infested grain stores. Inevitably, some of the cats—perhaps the most gentle cats and those that begged for food—were adopted as pets. Domestication and selective breeding had begun. Enjoying the considerable benefits of human companionship, the wild cat willingly became tame. Your pet cat is a beggar and expects you to provide regular meals. He no longer needs to be a good hunter to survive. It is quite natural for you to enjoy the fact that your cat depends on you for the necessities of life. The reliance behavior is being perpetuated through intervention in breeding, and, in time, the cat's ability to hunt successfully will diminish, and an exaggerated dependence on humans will develop.

"When looking needy, I don't have to speak."

Silent survivor
Until recently, cats were reviled in the Singapore peninsula. The immigrant cats therefore evolved into small and silent scavengers rather than ardent beggars.

Reacting with fear
He may look sweet, but this feral kitten, never previously touched by people, reacted viciously when first approached. He soon relaxed and is capable of being socialized to humans.

"I know there's something good in here."

Nose receptors eagerly search out new smells

Back foot is ready to spring if quick retreat is needed

Adapting to circumstances

There are no obvious physical differences between wild and domestic cats, but the latter has developed a longer intestinal tract to cope with a more varied diet. Domestic cats can also develop unusual tastes if encouraged to do so.

Mouth is open in begging miaow

"Stop teasing and just feed me now."

Kitten learns by observing her mother

Begging effectively

This kitten learned at an early age to demand milk from her mother. This behavior is perpetuated in the adult mother cat as she meows and reaches up to beg for food from her owner. Mimicking her mother, the kitten quickly learns how to survive.

Learning centers in the brain

AS A SKILLED HUNTER, the cat must depend on its detection mechanisms, and the parts of its brain that are associated with the senses are well developed. All the senses and the body's hormone-producing glands send information to the brain, where it is interpreted so the body can be instructed how to respond. The cat's nervous system allows the feline to react almost instantaneously to external stimuli. The brain also sends instructions to the master gland of the hormonal system, the pituitary, in the base of the brain. Because brain activity demands considerable energy, the brain receives 20 percent of the blood pumped by the heart despite accounting for only 1 percent of body weight. The cat's brain consists of billions of specialized cells (neurons), and messages move through a cat's brain at almost 240 mph (390 km/h).

Parietal lobe *Interprets information from senses*

Cerebrum *Site of consciousness*

Corpus callosum *Connects left and right hemispheres*

Occipital lobe *Interprets visual and sensory hair stimuli*

Temporal lobe *Behavior and memory site*

Cerebellum *Coordinates motor activity*

Pineal gland *Produces melatonin to control waking and sleeping*

Spinal cord *Carries information between brain and body*

Frontal lobe *Controls voluntary movement*

Olfactory bulb *Processes scents*

Hypothalamus *Secretes hormones and governs autonomic nervous system*

Pituitary gland *Coordinates and controls other glands*

The anatomy of the brain

Anatomically, the cat's brain is similar to that of other mammals. The cerebellum coordinates and balances the movement of muscles; the cerebrum—the largest part of the brain—governs learning, emotion, and behavior; and the brain stem connects to the nervous system. A network of cells called the limbic system is believed to integrate instinct and learning.

The role of hormones

Hormones produced in the brain control most bodily functions, such as governing the metabolic rate and stimulating the adrenal gland to produce cortisol in times of stress or danger. Production of sexual hormones, eggs, and sperm is controlled by follicle stimulating hormone in females and luteinizing hormone in males.

Do cats think?

Dr. Temple Grandin, an animal-behavior expert at Colorado State University's veterinary school, has autism, a neurological condition characterized by self-absorption and an inability to relate socially. She says that her disability gives her a unique understanding of the feline mind and that it's likely that, as many autistic people do, cats think through sensing, through pictures and memories of smells and sounds. Cats can certainly solve simple problems. The first hospitalization units I had at my veterinary clinic had two door latches, but many cats learned within hours how to open one with one paw and the other, simultaneously, with the other forepaw. I had to increase the distance between the latches to make the hospital units escape-proof. Cats, particularly kittens, learn best through observation. Kittens that watch their mother capture and kill mice are better mousers when they mature than those that have not had the opportunity.

Considering intelligence

Scientists are generally accepting of the idea that there are multiple forms of intelligence. For humans, intelligence manifests itself in eight different ways:

1. Linguistic
2. Logical-mathematical
3. Musical
4. Spatial
5. Bodily kinesthetic
6. Naturalist
7. Interpersonal
8. Intrapersonal

This concept of human intelligence can be adapted to studying cats. The last five forms listed above may be used to describe feline intelligence. I believe cats have learning centers in their brains to facilitate these abilities. For example:

■ An excellent capacity to map comparatively large territories—form 4
■ A natural knowledge of motion and forces: understanding mechanics—form 5
■ An ability to choose where to live, both for safety and for productivity—form 6
■ An acute understanding of danger, self-defense, and how to be cautious—form 6

■ An ability to know and remember what should and should not be eaten—form 6
■ An innate understanding of the behavior of other animals, including a capacity to predict their likely behavior from their initial actions—form 7
■ An intuitive inclination to patrol, investigate, and mark territory—form 7
■ A recognition of the role and importance of kinship, especially the maternal relationship—form 7
■ An understanding of the importance of personal hygiene—form 8.

Physical dexterity
Better than any other domesticated species, cats use fine motor skills to control the muscles of their paws. Instead of grasping with opposable thumbs as primates do, cats use their extendable claws to grasp and hold.

Breed evolution

THE DESCENDANTS of the North African wild cat were first cherished as domestic pets in their native lands in about 1000 BC. Merchants then discovered that cats were good traveling companions, able to decimate a ship's rat population. They were also valuable commodities because they fetched high prices in foreign lands. As the merchants sailed the trade routes, so cats spread around the world. Breeding was, of course, restricted to other cats within the same imported group, so the physical and temperamental characteristics that the merchants had originally selected were perpetuated. Merchants often singled out cats with blue, chocolate, and other non-agouti coats to take with them on their journeys. (A non-agouti coat is made up of hairs that are uniform in color from root to tip.) Cats possessing these coat colors were possibly less intimidated by humans and also less aggressive. The cats interbred in their new environments, creating gentler, tamer personalities.

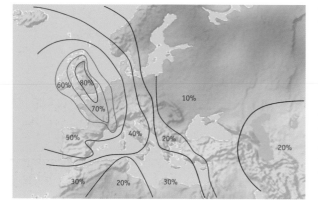

The tabby trail
The blotched, or classic, tabby pattern occurs in less than 20 percent of the cats living in northern Africa. The incidence of this pattern increases as the old trade routes are followed through Europe, reaching up to as high as 80 percent in some areas of Britain, the end of the old trade routes.

Markings rare in northern Africa

Striped tabby
The mackerel, or striped, tabby is now rare, although it was the original pattern of the northern African domesticated cat. Today, most tabbies have some blotched pattern too.

Blotched tabby
This blotched tabby pattern is uncommon in northern Africa. Traders were attracted to the cats with the most unusual coats to take with them on their ships.

Following trade routes
The North African wild cat has the potential to produce descendants with many fur colors, such as this blue-and-orange coat. The farther the distance traveled from northern Africa, the greater the incidence of unusual colors.

Plain colors
Cats with uniformly colored coats were originally rare, but through selective breeding they are now abundant. Such coats may be a "self," or solid, color, or a mixture, resulting in a "smoke" pattern.

Founder effect

A classic "law" of genetics says that the relative frequency of specific characteristics, such as coat color, in a randomly breeding population remains constant from one generation to the next. But if a small population becomes isolated, a phenomenon called "genetic drift" occurs, in which a gradual shift in gene frequencies is seen. The first cats to arrive on the west coast of Norway included ones with the uncommon coat-color combination of orange and white. The "founder effect" increased the frequency of that coat color in that isolated region of the feline world.

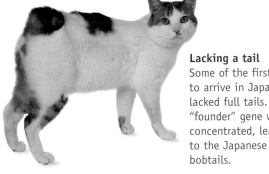

Lacking a tail
Some of the first cats to arrive in Japan lacked full tails. The "founder" gene was concentrated, leading to the Japanese bobtails.

Harmless variation
Instead of the normal five toes, polydactyl cats often have as many as seven toes on their forepaws.

What is intelligence?

WHILE IT IS EASY to talk about feline intelligence, it can be frustratingly difficult to define what is meant by the term. Cognitive psychologists have varied theories about different forms of intelligence, and these can be modified for determining how smart cats really are. Some behavior experts believe that cats "think" by sensing through pictures and memories of smells and sounds. It has been shown that kittens learn best through observation. For example, those that have the opportunity to see their mother capture and kill mice grow up to be better mousers than those that do not.

Core emotions

In his book *Affective Science: The Foundations of Human and Animal Emotions*, Professor Jaap Panksepp studied the core emotions, or "instinctual mechanisms," of rage, fear, separation distress (panic), play, lust, and caring at the brain level of a small mammal. He describes how play activity releases opioids in the brain and how the brain's frontal lobe grows as a response to playing behavior. The studies show how chemical systems in the brain regulate emotions, feelings, and social bonds, and that consciousness is built into the cat's value systems.

Short-haired coats are closer to original African coats

"I feel nice and warm even in winter."

Long-haired coats adapted for colder climes

The intelligence to adapt
Some 4,000 years ago, domestic cats inhabited only a small area of northern Africa. They began to disperse around 3,000 years ago, and the only ones to survive were those able to cope with the demands of a new environment. One very visible way in which cats have adapted to new surroundings is through the length of their coats.

Sleeping and dreaming
While he is asleep, your cat may flex his paws, twitch his whiskers, and give a flick of his tail; he may even mutter or growl. During deep sleep, electrical impulses in his brain are as active as when the cat is awake, so it is likely that cats dream, just as we do. On average, cats rest for around 18 hours a day, and it has been suggested that this is when they rehearse body actions, such as the fight-or-flight response.

"I know just how much space I need."

Ears are fully rotatable to pick up sounds from far afield

Eyes are adaptable to wide range of light conditions

Spatial awareness

When it comes to spatial awareness, bodily kinesthetic intelligence, and naturalist intelligence, cats are far more "intelligent" than both us and our other favorite animal companion, the dog.

"Don't worry— I'll take care of you."

Maternally minded

In cats, as with all mammals, the care and attention a mother affords her young is a form of instinctive behavior. Feeding, licking, and carrying young are all linked to intelligence.

2 STARTING A FAMILY

While most dogs are born at dog kennels, the majority of kittens are born in our homes, in litters that are often the results of unplanned pregnancies. One consequence is the regrettable ever-increasing number of kittens in need of good homes, but another is that these births give us and our families a ringside seat on the natural world—an unrivaled opportunity to observe both motherhood and the evolution of kittens from newborn helplessness to dramatic dexterity within three months.

We may hear cats mating, but we seldom see the act. The female encourages males to mate with her by caterwauling and then indulging in feline foreplay. Several matings are needed to induce her ovaries to release eggs, and if she is not mated she will have another heat cycle, often a few weeks later. The pregnancy is usually unremarkable, with no outward signs other than a pinking of her nipples in the first month. In the second month, her belly enlarges. Around 60 days after mating, she finds a secluded place to give birth. In our homes this may be inside a closet or behind a sofa. The birth is silent, and as the mother produces each kitten, she licks the membranes from their bodies, stimulating them to take their first breaths, chews off the umbilical cords, eats the placentas, licks the kittens dry, and helps them find her milk. A few days later she moves the entire litter to a new, safe nest, free from the odors of birth.

A natural earth mother
This cat knows how to be a good mother, because of "instinct," her hardwired brain anatomy; her hormones, which trigger milk letdown and calm behavior; and the experience of previous pregnancies.

Cats are not naturally sociable with each other. The domestic cat evolved from lone hunters, individuals adapted to take care of themselves, without support from others. The first six months of life is the only time that a cat will live in a natural pack, within a social order of mother and siblings. From that experience, some cats become dominant while others may be treated as losers, as "pariahs," denied access to food by the rest of the family. In nature, these "runts" would die, but through our intervention they often survive and make affectionate companions. By six weeks of age, the litter will annoy the typical mother with its pestering demands. She denies them access to food, forcefully disciplines aggressive play (especially from her male kittens), and sows the seeds for the eventual disintegration of the "pack," which occurs when the male kittens are driven away.

At birth, kittens are virtually helpless, with only a few senses moderately developed, but they rapidly develop, both physically and mentally. By six weeks of age, taste, hearing, scent, and sight are well developed. It is during this time that kittens are most adept at learning by observing each other's behavior, and especially that of their mother. By 12 weeks of age, balance and agility are remarkably defined. What differentiates kittens from puppies is that, while pups remain clumsy for several more months, kittens are now able to live in a three-dimensional world, to climb, to walk on ledges, to jump down. They are capable of stalking prey, of escaping from danger, but also of serious mischief.

A temporary pack
The domestic cat evolved to live independently, and most adults are content without other cats. A true social order occurs only in kittenhood and is determined by who gets the most productive nipples.

Choosing a partner

ALTHOUGH ARRANGED MARRIAGES are now the norm for most purebred cats, when left to nature it is the female prerogative to select a mate. Tomcats might engage in bloody duels for the right to mate with a receptive female, but it is just as likely that she will choose the loser as the father of her litter. Females normally experience several ten-day cycles of sexual receptiveness each year, which are brought on by increasing daylight in early spring. Cats housed indoors in artificial light can be sexually active at any time of year. During her receptive phase, the female undergoes a personality change, becoming affectionate and lascivious.

"I'm gorgeous, and you want me."

1 Signaling sexual interest
By rolling provocatively, this female is indicating her availability. She may also knead with her front paws and call out. Even the most withdrawn female will give these bold signals.

Body is relaxed but not yet receptive to mating

2 Tentative approach
The male advances cautiously, while the female continues to roll. He avoids eye contact and is careful not to come too close to her too quickly. If he does, she might turn and swipe at him or run away.

3 Reducing tension
The male begins to groom the female behind her ears to relax her and make her less likely to respond aggressively to his advances. The mating initiative comes completely from the female.

"I'll whisper sweet nothings in your ear."

"I'm sensing the moment is near."

4 Sexual arousal
Seduced by his grooming, the female turns onto her front and stretches out. Then she raises her rump and swings her tail to the side. If the male touches her without invitation, she may swipe at him.

Relaxed expression signals that mating can be attempted

"I could still say no, you know?"

5 Confirming receptivity
The male confirms that the female is fully receptive by sniffing the odors from her vaginal discharge and her urine. Preparation for mating is a lengthy business, but the mating itself will be short.

Pricked-forward ears indicate apprehension

Mating

CATS DO NOT form pair bonds. When mating ceases, the female has nothing more to do with the male. She is not naturally monogamous, and if several eligible toms are available, she might mate with all of them. Unlike most other domestic animals, cats are induced ovulators, which means that the act of mating stimulates the hormone changes that trigger the release of eggs. Therefore, the more frequent the mating, the more likely it is that eggs will be fertilized.

Mouth is open in readiness to grip

1 Getting into position
With her ears back, the female appears fearful as mating begins. The male starts to mount carefully, opening his mouth wide, ready to grasp the back of her neck should she decide to try to attack him.

"All right, I'm about to grab your neck."

2 Penetration
Standing astride the female, the male "pedals" with his hind legs and then makes just a few pelvic thrusts. Mating is over within a few seconds, but he needs a firm grasp on the nape of her neck to prevent her from turning on him.

3 Withdrawal
The female shrieks as the male withdraws. Hooklike barbs on the male's penis cause genital irritation, thereby stimulating the chain of nervous and hormonal reactions that culminate in ovulation.

Ears are pinned back in fear

4 Male apprehension
At the moment of her piercing scream, the male instantly disengages and moves away. The female will often lash out at the male as soon as he releases her from the neck grasp.

The brotherhood

Mating may occur up to ten times an hour. It ends only when the male is exhausted, and he may be replaced by another suitor. A succession of males, known as "the brotherhood," await their turn. At the beginning of mating, the male makes the advances and is often rebuffed. After repeated matings the female beckons another male with a provocative display. Eggs are released from the ovaries 24 hours after successful matings.

5 Relaxing together
After mating, the female allows the male to sit near her. They will groom themselves in preparation for a subsequent mating.

"She even lets me stay beside her."

"Sure, you can stay there ... for now."

Pregnancy behavior

YOUR PREGNANT CAT should be allowed to lead a normal life. During the early stages of pregnancy, it is safe for her to venture out and hunt. Climbing can be dangerous when she is greatly distended, because the weight of the unborn kittens alters her center of gravity and affects her balance. She will be innately more careful, but the experienced mother adapts better to changes caused by pregnancy. An increased level of progesterone brings on "maternal behavior," and the expectant mother spends more time relaxing. Near full term, her estrogen level rises, and she will begin searching for a nesting site.

Constricted pupils indicate relaxed state

"I just can't seem to get comfortable."

Large tummy makes female pear-shaped

"No, I'm not fat—I'm pregnant."

Pregnancy is clearly visible in normally slender Oriental Shorthair

Showing signs
The large belly shows up very clearly on the characteristically healthy but lean body of this Oriental Shorthair mother-to-be. The average number of kittens in a litter is four, but Oriental cats tend to have larger litters.

Behaving maternally

Even before your cat starts gaining weight and looking pregnant, her appetite increases and she becomes less active. Closer to term, she will groom herself more frequently, especially her abdomen and genital areas. As birth approaches, she will spend more time in her chosen nest, impregnating it with her scent. This will help her soon-to-be-born kittens in their orientation toward home.

Preserving strength
To conserve the energy she will need to give birth, the expectant mother tends to sit and lie around more than before. An increase in the level of progesterone, the pregnancy hormone, causes this relaxed, maternal behavior.

Lying comfortably
The expectant mother adopts a prone position, allowing the load in her abdomen to be more evenly distributed and supported by the floor. She remains cautiously active until hormonal changes cause her to slow down and rest more.

Nipples are pink and obvious, in preparation for suckling

The unborn kitten

If you suspect your cat is pregnant, you can confirm the pregnancy by checking if the nipples are pink and the belly is increasing in size. Between four and five weeks after conception, you should be able to feel golf-ball sized swellings. Prodding or poking can damage the embryo or even induce a miscarriage, so any manual examination should be gentle. Your cat should also start to behave maternally. The pregnancy lasts for nine weeks. Halfway through gestation, the embryo is already a perfectly formed miniature kitten. It then develops rapidly and weighs around 3½ oz (100 g) at birth.

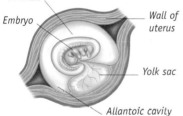

Amnion

Embryo

Wall of uterus

Yolk sac

Allantoic cavity

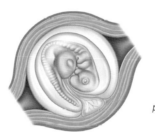

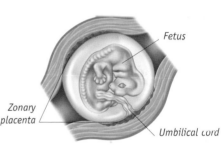

Fetus

Zonary placenta

Umbilical cord

At 16 days
The embryo is surrounded by fluid and is attached to the wall of the uterus.

At 18 days
Head, backbone, and tail are obvious. The embryo feeds off nutrients in the yolk sac.

At 21 days
The limbs are visibly forming, as are the eyes. Food comes via the umbilical cord.

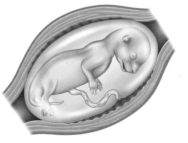

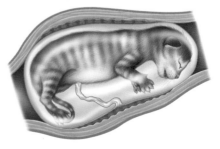

At 28 days
All the internal organs have developed. The tiny kitten is about 1 in (2.5 cm) long.

At 35 days
The developing fetus grows rapidly and is now about 2½ in (6 cm) long.

At 63 days
The kitten is ready to emerge. In the past 28 days it has doubled in length.

Giving birth

THE BIRTH is seldom very difficult. Any time between 60 and 70 days after mating, the mother's biological clock alters her hormone production, and labor begins. She will seek out the site chosen for the birth— a secluded, warm place with a surface she can dig at. Her breathing quickens, and she might start to purr rhythmically. As labor continues, she will usually produce a vaginal discharge and soon after will begin to strain. Once the contractions are occurring about every 30 seconds, a delivery is imminent. A resourceful and healthy mother will usually manage her birth without your help.

"No need to fuss—I can manage."

1 Labor begins
The kitten emerges from the birth canal in a lubricated sac. The mother has good control of her abdominal muscles, and she concentrates on pressing down to get the kitten out. Her leg lifts up out of the way.

Relaxed leg indicates easing of contractions

2 The birth
The kitten is born, and the labor pains ease, allowing the mother to bend to reach the amniotic sac and lick it away. Licking is a hardwired, or instinctive, response. The kitten is being born in a "diving" head-and-feet first position; about 70 percent of kittens are born this way.

Each kitten emerges in its own amniotic sac

3 Cleaning up

The mother tidies up the area around the newly born kitten, eating the amniotic sac. The kitten is helpless, and she licks her dry to prevent her from getting cold. At this point she is still attached by the umbilical cord.

"First, I'm going to clean you up."

Face is licked to clear mucus and facilitate breathing

4 The lick of life

The mother now licks the kitten's face to clear all the mucus from her nostrils and mouth. She is naturally vigorous and quite rough—the licking action must make the kitten gasp. The kitten's lungs will then inflate, and she will start to breathe freely.

Kittens orient themselves via heat receptors on the head

5 Hiding the evidence

After the birth of each kitten, the mother prepares herself for the next. She licks all the fetal fluids from her belly, around her genital area, and even from the floor. For the time being, she disregards those kittens that have been born.

Righting mechanism develops in the womb

After birth

FIRST LITTERS are generally smaller in numbers than subsequent ones. This is a practical reality considering that, for the birth of her first litter, the mother has only instinct to guide her. She knows what to do with the newborn kittens (and their afterbirths) because a mother's responses are hardwired into her brain. For subsequent births, she uses not only her hardwired "instinct" but also her learned experiences; this makes the later births ever more efficient. Experienced mothers are both proficient and successful at safely rearing large litters such as this one.

"Oh, there's just so much to do."

1 Two jobs at once
Lapsing in concentration, the mother licks one kitten while giving birth to another. Soon she will attend to the newborn, licking away the membrane. The more litters a cat has produced, the more competent she will be in the birth process.

Infanticide

Infanticide, the killing of the young of your own kind, is a horrible but natural behavior of some species, including some cats. It has been studied extensively in lions, where it is common—even normal—for a male lion taking over a pride of females to kill the young that were sired by other males. Contrary to some anecdotal stories, infanticide is not a natural behavior in the domestic cat. Because a litter can be sired by several fathers, there is no evolutionary reason for the practice to have developed.

2 Eating the afterbirth
The afterbirth, or placenta, is expelled, and the mother eats it to hide signs of the birth from predators. It gives her valuable nourishment, since she may not leave the kittens to find food for herself for the next few days.

3 Severing the cord
The mother chews off the umbilical cord about 1 in (2.5 cm) away from the kitten, using her side, or carnassal, teeth in a shearing action. An inexperienced mother may need help. Next, she cleans up all the bloody discharge.

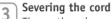

Mom curls up to bring kittens near her nipples for first feeding

"My kittens rely on me for everything."

Mom licks kitten's rump to stimulate bodily functions

4 Preparing the meal
Sometimes even before the last kitten has been delivered, the mother curls into a horseshoe shape, drawing the kittens toward her nipples with her paw. The kittens paddle toward the feeding station and nuzzle in to feed at the exposed nipples.

The first few weeks
Experiences such as contact with other animals during the first weeks of life are critical to a cat's future personality. This kitten is just a few months old, but his character was almost fully formed within his first seven weeks. In contrast, a puppy's nature is molded during the first 12 weeks of life.

Good mothering

THE INTERVAL BETWEEN BIRTHS can be as little as five minutes or as long as two hours. With very large litters, the mother may deliver only some of the kittens and settle down, exhausted, to feed them. She will then go into labor once more, up to 24 hours later, to give birth to the remainder of the litter. Newborn kittens are helpless and rely on their mother to provide food, protection, and warmth. She is instinctively maternal and will start to lick and feed them as soon as they are born, rarely leaving them during their first 48 hours of life.

Undivided attention
The mother cat responds to her kittens' cries by licking them as they burrow in for a meal. The last kittens to be born are still damp, but her licking has stimulated their breathing.

Pink feet indicate circulation is working well

Location of heat receptors, the kitten's most developed capacity

Mother pants from effort of labor

"I'm wiped out, but I'll defend my kittens."

Kittens snuggle together for warmth

Sibling Rivalry
In a large litter there is competition between the kittens. The rivalry is healthy, since it produces a creative environment. However, sometimes a loser, or "runt," emerges.

Do not disturb
The mother will be irritated if you disturb her and may hiss and spit. Staying close to her kittens, she pants with exhaustion. Soon she will relax and begin to feed them.

Sisters, mothers, and aunts

Collective upbringing is common within the matriarchal society of domestic cats, especially among feral urban cats that live near good food resources. A contingent of sisters, mothers, and aunts will look after a "daycare" of as many as 40 kittens, even suckling kittens that are not their own when necessary—in the absence of a hunting mother, for example. This form of upbringing provides intense social activity for the kittens.

Protecting the kittens

THE MOTHER BONDS QUICKLY with her newborns, and instinctively knows how to care for them. Even a first-time mother responds to her kittens' cries by retrieving them when they wander away. She is able to recognize each kitten in her litter by its distinct smell, secreted from skin glands on the head. Kittens rest only when they are huddled with their mother or with each other. Just when they appear to be accustomed to their new environment, the mother abandons the soiled nest and moves them to a safer site. This behavior stems from living in the wild, where it is necessary to move away from any signs of the birth, which might encourage dangerous predators.

Defenseless at birth
The newborn kitten is unable to see, hear, or walk. She uses the heat receptors on her face to help her seek out her mother.

Delicate mouthful
The mother moves from the soiled nest when her kittens are four days old. She carries one at a time, grasping each one in her jaws, while the kitten stays relaxed and passive.

Wide-jawed grasp carries kitten safely

Settling in

The mother is happy and relaxed in her new nesting site and seems oblivious to the kittens crawling all over her. The young kittens are drawn to their mother by the warmth of her body.

Boldest kitten feeds first

"It looks rough, but I'm gentle, really."

Kitten carried without harm

Hind legs flex; tail turns up

Traveling position

The kitten remains passive and assumes a fetal position as she is carried to the nest. Later in life, cats adopt the same tuck position when picked up by the scruff of the neck.

Striding out

The mother "walks tall" when carrying the kitten in her mouth to reduce the danger of bumps and jolts. If the distance between nests is great, she may move her litter one at a time to a midway rest station, and then on to a new home.

Nursing

MOTHERS ARE VERY CALM when feeding their kittens, an influence of the pregnancy hormone progesterone. This hormone stimulates milk production and gives the mother a voracious appetite. The first milk that she produces, the colostrum, protects the kittens from many diseases. During the first days, the kittens' senses develop rapidly. They learn the scent of their chosen nipple and quickly develop a preference for it. Usurpers often give up suckling when an owner claims his preferred nipple.

Eyes open
The kitten, now six days old, has opened his eyes. Although controlled genetically, kittens reared by young mothers or in dark dens open their eyes earlier than normal.

Ears will not open until around the tenth day

Eyes open between four and ten days

Suckling for comfort

A kitten's need for milk peaks at around three weeks of age, at which time its mother introduces it to solid food. By six weeks of age, it is weaned off mother's milk and now survives solely on solids. However, kittens continue to suckle, albeit for comfort and security rather than nutrition. Comfort suckling is normal until ten or more weeks of age.

"I'm totally chilled out."

Total relaxation
The hormone progesterone, which causes the milk to flow, leaves the mother contented. The constricted pupils indicate that her state of arousal is low.

Mother pushes kittens toward nipples

1 **Milk station**
Nipples toward the rear of the mother have the most abundant milk supply. They are claimed by the more dominant kittens, who usually grow to be strong and secure.

2 **Jockeying for position**
For the first few weeks, the kittens are totally dependent on their mother to position herself so that they can suckle. Unwittingly, the mother prevents the runt from feeding when she stretches out her paw.

Most productive nipples are in abdominal region

Kitten lets go after feeding

3 **Drinking time**
There is a limit to how long the kittens may feed. The mother starts to get up, forcing the kittens away. The kitten that has not fed wanders off. The mother is watchful, but she will show concern only if she hears a distress call.

Fostering

FOSTERING IS NOT A BY-PRODUCT of human intervention in cat breeding. It is a natural feline behavior that allowed some mother cats to leave the den to hunt while others took over the nursing. For several days after birth, the cat's mothering instinct is so powerful that she readily fosters needy kittens, especially when they are only a few days old. The very young kittens do not discriminate, and willingly take any available comfort and nourishment. Foster kittens will compete with the kittens from the natural litter for the most productive nipples and, like cuckoos in the nest, may even usurp smaller or less dominant kittens.

The foster mother
This Burmese feeds her own Tonkinese kittens, as well as the two sealpoint Siamese that were introduced to the family when they were only a few days old. The foster kittens have settled in well and are competing with the mother's kittens for food.

Kitten struggles to latch firmly on to a nipple

"Wow, this is becoming a free-for-all."

Two foster kittens suckle at best nipples

Plenty for everyone
The Tonkinese kitten has now found a nipple, which she will defend for herself. Her mother continues to feed all the kittens until it is time for weaning. Fostering usually prolongs milk production, since the additional suckling stimulates milk flow.

Hand-rearing

You can hand-feed an orphaned kitten on a special milk formula using a dropper. The kitten will receive nourishment, but unless he is brought up with other cats, he will lack vital social contact from other kittens and his nursing mother. This can result in emotional deprivation, and the kitten may not develop a cat's social graces. When an adult, he is likely to be a poor breeder. When hand-rearing, you must also wipe the anogenital region with moist tissue to stimulate evacuation.

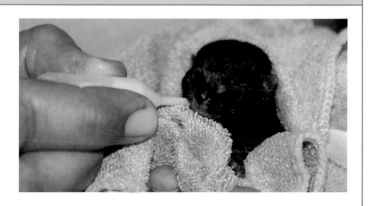

Sealpoint Siamese have darkened "points" on ears

A temporary family unit

These kittens have formed a close-knit group, just like a genetically related "normal" litter, huddling together for security and the warmth of body contact. Growing up as a foursome will provide them with more opportunities for both mental and physical activities.

"Just hanging out with my brothers."

Developing senses

AT BIRTH, the only sensory abilities that are nearly, or sometimes completely, mature are heat sensation and smell. But by three weeks of age, the other senses are on their way to total development. The voice starts to develop its range of adult sounds—initially distress sounds, but soon threatening sounds too. The ability to scent and to taste develop rapidly, as does vision and hearing. In order to be a successful hunter and to protect itself, a kitten must also develop its brilliant sense of balance—the ability to live in a three-dimensional world.

Distress call
With mouth wide open, this anxious kitten cries for her mother. The voice is functional from birth, and the kitten uses the distress cry when hungry, trapped, cold, or isolated from her mother or siblings. Mothers soon learn to identify the cry of their own kittens.

Sleeping with you

Under normal circumstances, almost the only time that cats sleep in contact with other cats is when they are kittens. With maturity comes separation from the family, and independence. If, during a kitten's early learning, it discovers that people are safe and successful "mother substitutes," it may sleep next to them into adulthood. While cats that are well socialized as kittens take pleasure in acting as hot-water bottles, rescued feral cats seldom do.

Fluid in eye is cloudy until five weeks of age

"I don't really see so well just yet."

Heads down and sniffing
Curiosity develops early. These kittens are using their sense of smell to explore their surroundings. Smell is the first sense to develop completely and is the most developed at birth.

Tail is held erect to help with balance

"I know she's close—I can smell her."

"Nice and easy, taking baby steps."

One paw raised at a time for stability

Claws cannot retract at this age

A sense of balance
The three-week-old kitten has just mastered walking. Still learning to balance, he is rather clumsy. Tentatively picking up one paw at a time, he makes steps with widely placed feet. Although the touch receptors on the paws are developed, the brain cannot fully integrate the stimuli.

Learning the ropes
A kitten's senses rapidly mature. Balletic balance gives it an early opportunity to explore the three dimensions in which it will live as an adult. By eight weeks of age, it can extend its claws to grasp and climb. By 12 weeks, it has all the sensory abilities of an adult cat.

Relying on Mother

CURIOSITY DEVELOPS IN KITTENS much earlier than fear, and once they can walk, they will investigate any new sight, sound, or smell. Although they quickly become gregarious and inquisitive, young kittens remain overwhelmingly dependent on their mother for feeding, cleaning, and rescuing from danger. It is left to Mother to observe her kittens' activities and to take them back to safety if she feels they are at risk. Until the kittens are about six weeks old, she is their only source of nourishment, providing them with all the necessary contact for full physical and emotional development.

Close quarters
This seven-week-old kitten still thrives on physical contact with her mother. The mother's facial expression shows that she is slightly annoyed at being used as a jungle gym.

Food and security
At six weeks, the kittens no longer depend on their mother's milk for nourishment, but they still continue suckling. They compete with each other for a nipple and enjoy the security of being with their mother as she relaxes. Weaning kittens earlier than six weeks will restrict their emotional development.

Vigilant mother
Mom always keeps a watchful eye on her litter. Here she retrieves a straying kitten. As the kitten grows, the skin becomes looser and the neck grasp gets more difficult.

Wool sucking

Kittens suckle for nourishment for six weeks, and then for comfort for another four to six weeks. If they are taken from their mothers too soon, before completing their "comfort suckling" stage, kittens may perpetuate their need to do so by kneading on your sweater or on your skin, to "release milk," and by sucking on skin such as earlobes or on wool.

"Right, let's clean you lot up."

Sanitation unit
For the first three weeks, the mother licks the kittens' anogenital regions to stimulate them to urinate and defecate. She also consumes all their bodily discharges.

Early exploration
This precocious four-week-old kitten is already venturing out on his own, fearlessly exploring his surroundings. The mother stands by, observing his progress.

Learning to move

KITTENS CAN CRAWL from birth. Heat receptors on the nose tell them where to find their mother. At two weeks the brain is receiving information from the other senses to help develop fluid movement. At seven weeks the kitten moves like an adult, and by ten weeks he will be able to walk along narrow ledges, such as the top of the garden fence, balancing perfectly. Messages from each of the senses are sent to the brain.

The coordinating center in the brain interprets these messages, then sends further instructions to the appropriate muscles. The messages travel very fast, enabling the cat to operate fluidly. The forelimbs move freely, and because the center of gravity is closer to the head, most of the activity comes from the front. Hind legs provide rapid acceleration and the tail acts as a rudder.

1 Paddling
At ten days the kitten scrambles along with her belly on the ground, paddling with her limbs. Her head is like a battering ram and is used as a probe to locate the warm nest.

Tummy drags along ground

Heat receptors on nose leather are extremely sensitive

Tail held high for balance

2 Flat feet
The kitten can balance at two weeks but cannot yet walk easily. Although able to support her body weight on her limbs, she will topple over if she lifts more than one limb at a time. The feet are kept flat on the ground as she crawls along.

Entire foot on ground for balance

3 Walking tall
Increased mobility coincides with an increased curiosity. At three weeks, the kitten's hind legs are in the tiptoe "sprinter's position." She can support her entire body weight and place her feet, but not yet exactly where she wants them.

On tiptoes is the cat's natural position

"I'm getting the hang of this!"

Tail is still raised for balance

"Okay, now— I'm walking here."

Paw reaches out confidently

Tail is now in lower position

"I'm becoming quite expert at this."

4 Confidence building
The kitten still has to concentrate hard on where to place her feet, but she is unlikely to tip over at four weeks of age. The organ of balance in the ear is developed enough for stalking and chasing siblings and other objects.

5 The small adult
When five weeks old, the kitten moves fluidly. She does not need to concentrate so intently and is able to move naturally, mimicking her mother. The tail drops because it is no longer needed as a rudder.

6 Complete agility
The kitten has learned all the movements necessary for survival by the time she reaches ten weeks. She can stride confidently along a branch, with no danger of falling. Still small, she now has all the characteristics of a fast, agile, and silent hunter.

Leaps and bounds

DESIGNED TO BECOME HUNTERS, kittens rapidly develop an enviably fluid and graceful agility. This enables them to alter the position of their bodies and catch unsuspecting prey at a moment's notice. At six weeks their balance is better than a human's will ever be. This is because a large part of the cat's brain is devoted to receiving and interpreting messages from the organ of balance and from the eyes. The skeleton—particularly the backbone and joints—and muscles are well adapted for pouncing, climbing, and balancing. Cats spend a lot of time on lookout duty, choosing trees, ledges, and rooftops for their observation posts. With all this climbing comes the risk of a fall, which is why cats need a superb sense of balance. If a cat falls, her body rotates in the air, turning her the right way up before she reaches the ground.

Boys will be boys

As with all mammals, the male kitten's brain is "masculinized" in the womb just before birth, when the kitten's testicles produce a short burst of male hormone. (The female kitten's brain, on the other hand, remains "neutral" until puberty.) Male kittens naturally play rougher games than females do, and by five months of age their boundless activity becomes so annoying that they are driven from the nest. This is how the matriarchal society is perpetuated.

Impromptu jump
Springing spontaneously into the air, the kitten twists at the waist to face the prey, bending the body into a U-shape. Extremely strong ligaments around the joints add extra thrust to the powerful thigh muscles.

Ready to pounce
The kitten creeps up on her prey and then, still keeping her hind legs on the ground, springs forward to catch it unawares. The pounce is the hunting maneuver that is used most frequently by a cat.

Planned leaping
Calculating to reach a particular point, the kitten uses powerful hind-leg muscles to make a series of half-bounds. She lands, balancing effortlessly, on her front feet.

Horizontal jumping
With paws at the ready to grasp the prey, the kitten leaps forward to cover distance, but she may also inadvertently scare away her victim.

"Whoa, I'm catching some serious air!"

Vertical leaping
All four feet lift off the floor as the kitten jumps up and back. Once airborne, he unsheaths his claws, ready to grasp on to anything. This type of leap is used later in life to catch birds and flying insects.

Crash landing
Not every movement is successful, but the kitten's acute righting reflex ensures that she will land upright. The paws are held far apart to help absorb shock.

Weaning

SOONER OR LATER, kittens become a nuisance to their mother. Exactly when this occurs varies from litter to litter. In general, however, kittens are completely weaned at seven weeks, but some mothers get fed up with the razor-sharp teeth much earlier than this. Other may continue to suckle for several more months, regardless of milk flow. In both instances, the need for independence eventually overcomes all kittens, and they relinquish the security of Mother to brave the perils and uncertainties of adulthood. First, the more assertive male kittens leave or are driven away by their mothers, then the females follow suit.

Mother remains
protective of
kittens for weeks

Separation begins
This six-week-old kitten no longer needs her mother's milk, but she will continue to stay close by for several more weeks yet.

"I'll suckle for as long as I can."

A head start in life

Nature understands how vital good nutrition is for the future health and well-being of kittens. A mother will starve her own body if necessary to ensure she produces sufficient nourishment for her kittens. By the time the kittens are weaned, mothers who have to find their own food may shrink, quite literally, to skin and bone. However, after weaning, the weight she lost is then rapidly regained.

Raised leg allows
kittens to suckle

Prominent shoulder
blade indicates depleted
energy stores

Cutting the apron strings
At six weeks, these kittens are still voracious feeders and
are becoming a physical drain on their mother. Their milk
teeth, which are very sharp, also cause her discomfort.

Forced independence
Annoyed by the persistent feeding demands, the mother
disengages from the litter and walks away. This distancing
herself is triggered by a drop in maternal hormone levels.

Breakfast call
Even though these kittens are of weaning
age, the mother takes the initiative and
gently licks them awake for breakfast.
Maternal care varies from mother to
mother, but the kitten's personality is
certainly influenced by her behavior.

Suckling for comfort
With only two kittens in her litter, this
mother has found feeding much less of
a physical drain than would be the
case with a large litter. At seven
weeks the milk has almost
dried up, but suckling is
a comfort behavior that
often continues beyond
seven weeks.

3 WHAT CATS DO

Cats listen to their own rhythms. Dogs, because they are so biologically sociable, are relatively easy to train to do unnatural things, such as pointing at prey but not capturing and killing it. Cats would never do such a silly thing. They do what cats have evolved to do, not what we tell them to do: compete for territory, hunt for food, and protect themselves from aggression, but also to be sociable with others, especially if the "others" are not other cats. Because people are not very catlike, we often make better companions for cats than other cats do.

The modern "pet" cat is a model of intentional arrested emotional development. Indeed, it is this precise fact that has been the key to its enormous increase in numbers in the latter part of the 20th century, when the cat superseded the dog as our most numerous home companion. All kittens—whether raised in our homes or in the absence of human contact—develop in similar ways. They form temporary bonds with their littermates, they play with each other, they enjoy body contact, and they hone their hunting skills by stalking each other. If people are integrated into these activities while the kittens are young, specifically when they are between three and seven weeks old, they will continue to pursue these activities with people throughout their adult lives. They may stalk our ankles, for example, but they will also enjoy playing with us and being stroked by us.

Meeting threats offensively
The cat is a superb hunter-killer, but it is also potential prey itself. To compensate, when under attack, a cat will arch its back to look larger, flatten its ears to protect them, and hiss like a snake.

Lifelong lessons
Kittens develop social relationships before the age of seven weeks. Raised from birth with species usually considered quarry, such as this squirrel, a cat will not prey on that species later in life.

In the absence of a human family, a kitten learns the skills needed to survive on its own, to compete for a home and hunting territory, to hunt successfully, and to avoid danger. The cat soon develops an early and confident independence. All cats, housebound or otherwise, instinctively understand offensive and defensive feline body language. They instinctively mark their hunting or resting territory with scent markers such as urine, feces, and cheek-gland rubs, as well as through the use of visual markers such as scratched posts or unburied feces. Outdoor cats tend to patrol their territories daily, leaving odor or visual signs of their presence. Indoor cats also need to carry out these same behaviors, and the normal activities of using scratching posts and spraying urine can lead to conflict with cat owners, who will often consider these normal feline behaviors to be problem behaviors.

Cats raised from kittenhood with people (or with other non-cat species) are perfectly capable of remaining sociable with people (or that other species) for their entire lives. Cats raised in the absence of human contact during the first seven weeks of life find it much more difficult to be sociable with people. They will eventually relax in the company of the people they know, but it is likely that they will have a lifelong wariness of strangers.

Playing for keeps
A kitten's offensive and defensive tactics, as well as its hunting skills, are developed through play. Littermates that live together into adulthood can retain a lifelong ability to play-fight.

Natural-born killer
The cat's natural prey is rodents, and given the opportunity, most cats are efficient hunters. Hunger and the need to hunt are different. The most successful hunters do so only for the thrill of the kill, rather than to satisfy hunger pangs.

Forming friendships

BETWEEN THE AGES of two and seven weeks, your kitten must be mentally stimulated if he is to mature into a secure and extroverted cat. Initially the kitten's social activity centers on his mother and gradually transfers to his siblings. At about two weeks, kittens start to play with one another, and this social interaction teaches them how to make friends. This playing gently introduces them to the concerns of adulthood. Play helps keep them together when their mother is absent, hunting for food. They practice aggressive gestures to establish which displays intimidate their siblings most effectively. Some aspects of play, such as biting the nape of the neck, rehearse sexual behavior; others train the kittens to hunt. The kittens will stalk and pounce as if preying on each other. Aggressive male-kitten play eventually leads to their banishment from the litter.

Flattened-back ears show play is more serious

Playful attack
The mother engages in playful advances from one six-week-old kitten while another suckles. As her kittens mature, she will become increasingly intolerant of their antics.

Fighting words
This six-week-old kitten backs off from a fight. Games that once ended amicably now often conclude with a glower and a hiss.

"I like swishy tails—they're lots of fun."

Rough and tumble
At three-and-a-half weeks of age, these kittens roll together and tussle. The sparring may look serious, but at this stage it is for fun. A hugging and licking session will usually follow this kind of play fight.

Face rubbing

Cats have scent glands on their lips and cheeks, and they "cheek-rub" this scent onto objects within their territory, such as upright posts, as well as on other members of their family or cats considered friends. Cats willingly mark us, too, by rubbing their faces, often followed by their entire body, against us.

"Hey, things look different from here!"

"Ow! Careful where you put those claws."

Creative play
The kittens are relaxed as one turns on her side to expose her tummy. Her sister plays with her tail, learning that she must react quickly to catch moving objects.

Play and contact

PLAY MIGHT APPEAR purposeless, but nature is seldom frivolous. Each aspect of the kitten's play has significance. Play with toys begins at three weeks, when the youngster paws at movable objects. Soon he will be batting, holding, and exploring anything that makes him curious. If he is introduced to humans at this age, he willingly plays and, when he grows older, he will be happy to be part of the family. Both types of play are a means of preparing the kitten for the adult world.

Moving targets
The kittens watch the ball to see if it moves. The orange kitten touches it inquisitively. As the ball rolls, he stalks it like prey. Learning that a ball rolls silently is as important as learning that breaking a twig makes a noise.

"What are you looking at over there?"

Hunting skills
The tabby focuses his attention on the ball. Such staying power suggests that he will develop into a good hunter. The orange kitten's concentration has wandered from the ball, and he now watches his sibling.

Ears prick forward to funnel in sounds

Kitten stares at the ball

"That ball. It moved without a sound."

Object play

In playing with different objects, such as leaves, or toys, such as small balls, kittens learn about their environment. If they are to hunt prey successfully, they must be aware of how things move, react, or make a noise when touched. The brain and connections between brain cells develop more in young kittens that are allowed to play than they do in kittens deprived of object play.

Learning to play ball
Small balls are favorite toys because they appear to run away. At eight weeks, the kitten has full control over the use of his paws and clasps the ball tightly. Like a small child, he is not prepared to share the toy with his sibling.

Playing with humans
When kittens are lillle, you should play with them for at least 40 minutes every day to ensure that they grow into relaxed and friendly cats. Frequent handling will make the kittens less fearful and more curious.

Feline greetings
Cats of all ages greet each other nose to nose. Cats that were socialized with humans (or dogs) as kittens will greet us (and our dogs) in a similar fashion. Cats also commonly greet us by rubbing their bodies against us—a behavior they seldom use when meeting other cats.

Competition

SOON AFTER THEIR EYES OPEN, kittens begin to tussle with each other. At first the rivalry is playful, but the clumsy paw-blows herald the more serious ranking disputes of later life. Eventually, the quickest-witted, strongest, or most outgoing kitten becomes dominant. At first the litter appears to live together without friction and with equal rights. At dinnertime, all the kittens gather around Mom with no regard as to who should eat first. Ranking in kittens is not as pronounced as in puppies, but a hierarchy does develop. In play, the role of dominant kitten is freely exchanged, but kittens soon learn that they can dominate others, or conversely, that submission is the most practical response to a sibling who is playing more seriously.

"You're no threat to me, little kitty."

Paw is drawn back, ready to deliver blow to aggressor

Stalking circle
These kittens circle, trying to sniff each other's anal regions. This is a classic rehearsal for the territory and rank disputes that occur later in life. Cats that know each other sniff noses.

Fixed stare unnerves rival

1 Dominant stare
All the play moves are identical to those of hunting or fighting. This kitten stares confidently at her sibling, just as she will later stare at prey. She will stay as still as a statue, hiding any intent, until finally one kitten forces the other to make a move.

2 Play attack
The kitten standing up is still acting dominantly, and judging by the erect fur on her tail, she is more serious about the game than her sibling. With no fear, the kitten on the ground rolls over to expose her tummy. In this instance, "belly-upping" is a play sign of submission.

"There's no need to be like that!"

Ears drawn back in fear

Ear position indicates contentment

3 **Escape route**
Suddenly the kitten that was playing realizes that her sibling is serious. The game has evolved into a hierarchy dispute, and so, with ears pinned back in fear, she retreats. Although the other kitten is lying down, the ear position indicates that she has won the challenge.

Tail fur is on end, indicating excitement

"Now look who's in trouble."

Sitting on hind paws gives position of superiority

Hunting skills

SOME BEHAVIORISTS BELIEVE that play behavior and hunting are manifestations of the same instinct. But this does not explain why your cat will hunt for food and still continue to play like a kitten. Hunting behavior is developed by the time a kitten is five weeks old. At that age, kittens use three different hunting maneuvers—the "mouse pounce," the "bird swat," and the "fish scoop"—and it is not long before they learn that there is action in the air as well as on the ground. Most kittens become excellent mousers, but due to relatively poor cat camouflage in many backyards, few will mature into expert bird-catchers, so their effect on bird populations would appear to be limited.

Bird swat
This six-week-old kitten is still too young to do a real bird swat, but with claws out ready to grasp, she extends her paw to reach up at the unexpected movement in the air. When she is older, she will be able to leap into the air from a standing position.

"I've got you now, little birdie."

Balance for hunting
This six-week-old kitten balances on her hind paws to bat airborne objects, but she lacks the muscle coordination to leap. Her tail sticks out straight behind her to help with stability.

"You can run but you can't hide!"

Kitten has her claws unleashed in readiness

Tail is raised in excitement

Fish scoop
This kitten practices the flipping action that can be used to scoop a fish out of the water. She does not need her mother to teach her this gesture, since it is instinctive.

Bringing back the spoils
Once captured, prey must be carried away, even if it is only a fluffy toy. This kitten brings her toy chick back to the den just as her mother will bring back mice for the kittens.

Bird vs. rodent hunting

Though mature cats are not good at learning by observation, kittens certainly are. The instinct to hunt is inherited, but kittens learn hunting skills early in life by watching and copying their mothers. This is why successful bird hunters produce new generations of good birders. German ethologist Paul Leyhausen says that mothers not only show their kittens how to hunt but also use their voices to indicate what species of prey is being brought back to the den for them.

Flexible spine allows unexpected movement

"Surprise! Check out my moves."

Stalker behavior
This nine-week-old hunter has mastered the technique of stealthily creeping up on her prey. Kittens start stalking each other when they are only three weeks old, and they begin to stalk objects a short time later.

Mouse pounce
The stiff-legged sideways leap is a favorite maneuver of the nine-week-old kitten, practiced here on a fluffy toy. She springs down onto her "victim" rather than jumping up. Later in life, she may use this move to catch rodents.

Unusual friendships

FROM THE AGE OF TWO WEEKS, a kitten can also start to form relationships with prey (squirrel), predator (dog), or competitor (fox). Provided the kitten can play with and head- and flank-rub the stranger without being frightened away, it does not seem to matter where an animal fits in the cat hierarchy. Such friendships can be lifelong, but the period during which these bonds may form is short-lived, lasting no more than five weeks. The permanent fear a cat has of other species— for example, a fox or dog—and the instinct to prey on small species—such as a mouse or rat—does not develop until after the kitten is seven weeks old. Studies show that when kittens are raised to six weeks old with rats, they refuse to prey on that breed of rat later in life. But if the first meeting is delayed beyond seven weeks, the relationship turns into one of hunter and hunted.

Exploring the differences
This kitten enjoys a relaxed relationship with the fox cub. Until he is seven weeks old, the kitten looks upon different species simply as other kittens or as cats that either smell or look different.

Hierarchy play
The kitten and fox cub play a game of dominance and submission in the same way that kittens play together. Here, the kitten is feigning aggression by rolling over to expose teeth and claws.

Constricted pupils show kitten is not frightened

Ears are folded back into angry position

"Mind if I just perch up in here?"

Dog is curious but perfectly at ease

Breed differences

It was first suggested in the 1970s that different breeds or, indeed, different colors of cats were either more or less likely to accept strange new cats into their homes. In the 1980s and 90s, breeders and owners were surveyed on the subject. While there were no reported differences according to coat color, Siamese and Asian cats were consistently reported to be less likely to accept unrelated new cats into their households, while Persian cats were more likely than average to accept the presence of a new feline.

Befriending the enemy
Showing no fear, this kitten clambers up onto the dog to seek out warmth and security. Gentle adult dogs or puppies less than 12 weeks old are ideal for these early social meetings.

Fear of the unknown
Slightly fearful yet inquisitive, this kitten has his hackles partly raised and his back arched as he investigates the squirrel. There is great curiosity about small species that are the size of prey.

"It's okay— I'm not going to eat you."

Hind legs are free to kick

Mock attack
The kitten attacks the squirrel playfully, but he will not "bite home." Furthermore, it is unlikely that the kitten will kill squirrels when he is older. In turn, the squirrel is not frightened because it was raised with cats.

Learning to survive

KITTENS ARE TAUGHT how to catch and kill prey by their mother. This is an essential skill for feral cats, but even your pet cat will teach her kittens how to find and hunt for food, despite the fact that you usually provide regular meals in a food bowl. To begin with, the kittens must learn to identify potential victims, so initially the mother brings prey home dead. Next, the kittens must learn how to kill, so she returns with live prey. At first the kittens may be apprehensive and fearful, but they soon become brave enough to chase and capture chosen prey, throwing it before finally making the kill. Kittens raised by a mother that is a successful hunter are more likely to become successful hunters themselves, since a good teacher passes on her skills. However, kittens can still become adept hunters without training from their mother.

1 Providing prey
This mother has killed a mouse for her kittens to play with. Her rigid stance and dilated pupils show that she is excited. She uses vowel sounds to tell the kittens that she has a mouse or, perhaps, a rat that may put up a fight.

2 Careful examination
Under Mom's watchful eye, the kittens examine the dead mouse. By mimicking their mother's behavior, the kittens learn to use all their senses to investigate the rodent. Its scent will become a lifelong memory.

"I wonder what she's got for us today."

Making demands
This pet cat stands up and begs for food. By watching and listening to her mother, the kitten also learns to beg and make the demand call. Through domestication, the feral cat has evolved from independent hunter into scavenger-beggar.

3 Preparing to eat
While the mother grooms one of her kittens to distract it, the other kitten concentrates on the mouse, holding it in her forepaws and kicking with her hind legs.

4 Playing with prey
Unfamiliar prey stimulates this kitten to play with her quarry rather than simply kill and consume it. The old story that a hungry cat kills more rats is inaccurate, because hunger motivates only the most experienced of hunters.

Eating habits

The natural prey for cats is small rodents. A cat's canine teeth are perfectly shaped to kill a mouse with a single bite through its spinal cord. Most cats stalk birds, but they do so inefficiently. However, when birds are the most readily available—or only—meals, cats adapt well as bird eaters. Worldwide studies confirm that, wherever they live, cats are true opportunists, adapting their eating habits according to what is locally available. This British cat has developed a taste for slowworms.

"Oh, this is so much fun. I love mice!"

The supreme hunter
The cat's ears funnel and pinpoint sound. Its nose scents prey, and its enormous eyes are able to capture the slightest movement. Camouflaged in natural colors and capable of perfect stillness, the domestic cat retains all the attributes of one of nature's most efficient hunters.

Becoming independent

IN THE WILD, where kittens do not experience contact with humans, they mature into lone hunters. There is no incentive to continue the group activity that existed when they were kittens. Independence is often asserted dramatically when the mock aggression of early play determines rank order within the litter.

By the time the kittens are 18 weeks old, the fights are serious, although the combatants rarely suffer any permanent injuries. The bonds of kittenhood are now broken and the litter disbands. Your kitten continues to accept close contact with you because she regards you as a mother substitute, not a littermate.

Tail is held high in excitement

"Get out of my personal space."

Forelimb outstretched for battle

Claws are extended for attack

1 **Play fighting**
When fully mobile, at about nine weeks, kittens will start to rehearse aggressive displays. With claws extended, the dominant kitten stands up, ready to pounce. Her sibling is lying down, thinking that the attack is in fun. But it is for real, and the game may degenerate into a serious fight.

Hind paw is firmly planted on the ground

REGALADO PATRI

37242001761829

5/29/2018

2 Neck bite
The submissive kitten suddenly realizes her opponent is serious. She leaps up from the prostrate position and launches a counterattack, trying to sink her teeth into her sibling's neck.

3 Lull in hostilities
At the age of nine weeks, the kittens may pause and relax during a fight. The kitten that was mauling assumes a less aggressive stance, while her sibling scrutinizes her, anticipating more activity.

Feral cat density

The need for independence partly depends on the availability of food. In the Scottish Western Isles, where food is scarce, there are three to five cats per square mile, and all kittens soon become independent hunters. Around fish-processing plants on the coast of Japan, however, unlimited resources lead to more than 2,500 cats per square mile, and female kittens stay within a matriarchal society.

"Here I come, ready or not!"

Folded-back ears indicate aggression

Ears are drawn back for protection

4 Aggression resumes
The kitten that was initially dominant makes a flying assault on her sibling, who starts to roll over so that she can defend herself from attack with her claws and teeth.

Being defensive

YOUR CAT IS MORE CONCERNED with defending her personal territory than with forming lasting friendships with other cats. Compared to a dog, she is a far less sociable creature and is remarkably adept at giving "go-away" signals. When your cat feels that she has lost control of the situation or that she is under threat, the "fight-or-flight" response is usually triggered and adrenalin is released. Your cat will stand her ground and give a show of aggression. Her hackles rise, her back arches, her tail bristles, her pupils dilate, and she may hiss and spit. Even a terrified cat will put on a convincing display of defensive body language, although in many cases such behavior masks fear rather than genuine aggression.

Sideways stance creates illusion of greater size

"I'm acting tough to scare you away."

Acting tough
With bristling tail, arched back, and hair standing on end, this cat is very scared but is trying to hide her fear with aggressive body language. Presenting herself side-on for maximum impact, she appears to be considering an attack on the opposition.

Firmly placed paws prepared for flight

*Tail fur stands
up slightly*

"You know,
I'm ready to
attack you."

"I'm big, and
you ought to
be afraid."

*Arched back appears
to increase size*

Weapons at the ready
Even though she is actually very frightened, this cat prepares
to act aggressively. Hissing, she starts to roll over so that
her teeth and claws are bared, ready to defend herself.

Pain could be the cause

Cats seldom complain when they are unwell. Their
self-preservation instinct compels them to behave as
normally as possible. If your cat routinely lets you
pick him up and unexpectedly becomes defensive
when you try to do so, it may be trying to conceal
that it is injured or ill and in pain. Seek veterinary
advice if your cat is unexpectedly defensive.

On the alert
This terrified cat is attempting to hold her ground.
Stimulated by adrenalin, her pupils have dilated and she
gives a direct stare to intimidate. Puffed up to a larger
size, she is staging a dramatic display of bravado.

On the offensive

THE ABILITY TO BLUFF with confidence is an absolute necessity for the cat that takes an offensive stance. There is no fixed pecking order in the cat world, so the tendency to act offensively or defensively varies according to the circumstances in which your cat finds himself. A cat in its own territory or holding the higher ground over an adversary—perhaps on a rooftop—will display offensive body language. Feeling confident, he is able to maintain full control of himself. Since, in this instance, the cat feels genuinely secure, the pupils do not dilate because the "fight-or-flight" response is not activated, as it would be in a frightened, defensive cat.

Secure at the top
While this cat sits on the roof, he dominates all others below him. Exuding confidence with his head, whiskers, perked ears, and smooth coat, the cat keeps a lookout for intruders. He may use his height advantage to ambush or attack.

Braving a rival
By putting her head forward, this bold cat refuses to be intimidated by the cat on the high ground. However, the erect fur on the tail is a sure sign that she is a little frightened.

Forward ears look assertive

"Brave—but I know you're scared."

Sweeping tail shows who is the boss

"Who, me? Scared? No way."

Dominant stance
Although watched by the queen below, this cat is not perturbed. With his well-developed sense of balance, he leans confidently over the post. Glaring down at the cat on the fence without worrying about falling off, he warns his adversary not to come any closer.

Tail fur begins to bristle with fear

Braced forepaws ready for action

Do cats hold grudges?

On occasion, after I have examined and treated a cat, and he is down off the examination table and walking around on the floor, and after he has thought about going off to hide in a corner, he walks back to me and bats my leg. In multiple-cat households, it is not uncommon for one individual to bat another as it walks past. Cats remember. Cats think about what previously happened and decide what to do in the future to prevent what happened from happening again. Some behaviorists say that this is simply a manifestation of dominant behavior, but I can't help but think it may also be a form of feline retribution.

Maternal anger
The mother's display of aggression frightens even the boldest of tomcats. She will not back off, and she threatens him by hissing and spitting offensively. If he does not retreat, she will spring forward.

> "Don't push your luck, buster."

Flattened ears show defensive anger

Fighting spirit
With ears slightly furled, the confident but angry cat opens her mouth wide to hiss or spit. The tongue is folded to funnel out a shot of hot breath. The lips curl back revealing sharp teeth, emphasizing the snarl.

Taut face muscles prepared for attack

Marking territory

THE FELINE LANDOWNER routinely leaves messages to tell other cats who owns the territory. This involves making regular patrols of his home ground and marking important hunting, feeding, and resting places. The marks he leaves can be either seen or smelled. The cat that rubs himself up against you is not simply showing affection. He is transferring his body odor, claiming you as part of his territory. When a cat has the freedom of the yard, he will scratch fence posts and tree trunks. Indoors, the cat may claw at sofas and chairs to make his mark visible. Both males and females can spray urine, even if they have been neutered, and a dominant tomcat will leave his droppings unburied as a combined visual and scent marker.

Ears are flattened back

Tail provides balance

Scratching posts
The ears fold back and an almost trancelike gaze comes over the cat as she reaches up to claw at the highest point possible. Wood is a favorite surface because it is not slippery. The scratches, which can be seen from a distance, are usually made in prominent sites.

Male cat's tail brushes its scent onto bushes

Cat pheromones

Natural body odors called pheromones influence behavior, but it was not until a French vet carried out detailed studies that these were synthesized and used clinically. Patrick Pageat collected and identified a series of different fatty-acid molecules secreted by the cat's cheek glands. He observed that two of these fatty acids had a calming effect on cats that were exposed to them. Pageat had these fatty acids synthesized by a French perfume company, and independent studies have confirmed their therapeutic value, especially in reducing urine-marking in multiple-cat households.

The indoor cat
Most females and neutered cats are content with a small indoor territory, but they still make marks. This neutered female has a chair that she vigorously defends.

"Now everyone will know this is my tree."

"Just letting you know I'm here."

Staking a claim
Urine spraying is a marking behavior and is completely different from emptying the bladder. The cat backs up to the object it intends to mark and, with a quivering tail, squirts urine straight out backward.

The face rub
The cat rubs her face against the fence to mark it. Scent from the cheek glands is transferred to the wood, giving a signal to other cats in the area that this is claimed territory, as well as other valuable information.

Urine is sprayed to mark. Anal gland squirts secretion onto droppings

Sebaceous glands secrete an oily substance with distinct smell

Glands on face produce a distinctive odor

The routine patrol
The cat must make fresh markings every day using bodily secretions. The marks left do not frighten away other cats. Rather, they tell intruders on the territory how recently the owner passed through.

Patrolling outdoors

MOST PET CATS ADOPT their owners' yards as their own territory. Because cats are so successful at adapting to human ways, surprisingly few problems arise from this arrangement. The size of a territory depends on the cat's age, sexual status, and personality. Females and neutered cats are usually content with fairly small land rights, while tomcats feel the need to patrol and defend much larger territories—often ten times the area of a female's. Feral toms and cats without owners also establish a hunting range connected to their home territory by specific boundary lines and pathways. If your cat does not have sufficient room in which to maneuver, he will remedy this by appropriating a neighbor's yard. He will stake it out with strategic droppings. Neutering dramatically reduces a cat's territorial demand because the sex hormone is one of the factors that drives the cat to create and defend territory.

Disease transmission

Infected wounds, particularly bite abscesses, are a common risk for all animals, both predators and prey. Cats are especially prone to abscessed bites from other cats, particularly when body language has not been sufficient to smother potential territory disputes. Other more dangerous microbes have adapted to the presence of concentrations of outdoor felines. As cat numbers increased, what were once relatively rare viral infections became much more prevalent. Both feline immunodeficiency virus (FIV) and feline leukemia virus (FeLV) are transmitted to other cats through their saliva via bites, but also through saliva left from being groomed by a carrier cat.

Cat sits comfortably in position of power

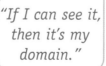

"If I can see it, then it's my domain."

Preserving land
Taking their cue from human territory markers, cats are often content to remain within one backyard but will vigorously defend that patch against other feline intruders. However, your cat's range may extend to more than one human territory.

Patrolling from above
Cats live in both the vertical and the horizontal world. Tomcats tend to spend more time policing their territory than females.

> "Hey! Why are you on my turf?"

Lowered hindquarters indicate apprehension

Holding the high ground
Regardless of which is the most dominant when two cats meet, the one that holds the highest ground has a distinct advantage. This is one reason why cats enjoy patrolling rooftops. From a height, your cat can survey his territory and shout insults at intruders.

Protecting the ideal home
A perfect home territory provides a reliable food supply and safe resting areas that are always accessible. The cat door ensures that your cat still retains some degree of independence, so he can come and go at will.

Adapting to human lifestyle
Many cats are content to live indoors with us, where there is no need to forage for food and where we "protect" the home territory. Even so, indoor cats will still assume ownership and defend a favorite spot, such as a chair.

The social cat

THERE IS NOTHING WRITTEN into a domestic cat's genetic code that prevents it from living contentedly with other cats, provided the conditions are suitable. Household cats willingly share territory when food is plentiful, and in such circumstances they need to communicate—not only to defend their territory but also to resolve differences of opinion and to maintain their status within the group. Unlike a wolf pack, a group of domestic cats has no distinct social hierarchy to which all members must adhere. This makes it much more difficult for behaviorists to interpret the social dynamics within the group.

This kitten's gaze settles on central dominant kitten

Group dynamics
Relationships within any group of cats are usualy quite fluid, but particular interactions can still be identified. In a small cat colony, for example, every cat will react in a different way toward each of the other group members.

"I'm REALLY not happy with you here."

Posture shows disdain at encounter

Mother cat allows kitten to rub against her

"Yes, I love you, too, my little one."

Who's the boss?
Domestic cats behave in your home much as they would in an outdoor colony. When two cats meet on "neutral" territory, the cat on higher ground is temporarily in charge; if they meet on level ground, the "dominant" cat may take a symbolic swipe at the "inferior" individual.

There's the rub
Cats frequently rub their bodies against each other, and which cat initiates this rubbing provides some clues about the hierarchical structure within a group. Kittens always start the process with their mothers, although once it has started, the mothers may rub their kittens in return.

People as cat substitutes

There is no denying that some of us get great pleasure not just from watching and living with cats, but also from caring for them. With their size, their soft sensuousness, and especially their large, staring eyes, they satisfy our inherent need to care for other living things. For some people, cats are genuine baby substitutes. (Some cat people argue that babies are cat substitutes!) But what are we to cats? To the social cat, people can make excellent cat substitutes. We are catlike enough to be played with and to give security, but sufficiently un-catlike so as not to be threatening or challenging. In many ways, to cats, people are much better to live with than other cats.

Expression indicates pleasure at being groomed

Feline bonding

Aggression is uncommon within a group or family and is reserved for "outsiders." Cats that are content in each other's company will sleep close together, or even in contact with each other, and will often groom each other. Mutual grooming cements feline relationships.

"There you go—all clean and tidy."

Making friends

Although the cat evolved as a lone hunter, a "selfish" individual interested primarily in itself, all that is needed to modify its independence is routine early contact with people. The cat's contentment with being "home alone" has rapidly made it our most populous companion.

4 BEING A CAT

It can be difficult to get into the mind of a cat, to think like a feline. While we share many of the same senses—sight, scent, taste, and hearing—not only are a cat's senses slightly different from ours, cats also have additional capabilities, such as the abilities to taste water, to scent sex (through the vomeronasal organ), to orientate, and to live comfortably in a three-dimensional world.

Your cat has retained all the skills of its North African ancestors. Cats hear better than we do, especially high-pitched squeaking sounds. They scent better—not only for the presence and freshness of food, but for dangers from other animals. Their large eyes not only dilate enormously, to allow in the maximum amount of light possible for hunting

at dawn and dusk, they also have highly reflective, mirrorlike membranes behind their retinas, to amplify available light. Conversely, in bright light, their pupils are capable of constricting to the merest slits, like an Inuit's snow goggles.

Using all the highly evolved skills of the successful small predator, cats observe the world around them more acutely than we do, noticing changes in our body language that we might not even realize we are making. Their dramatic range of voice and tone articulates their feelings and emotions, both to other cats and, of course, to us in ways that even we find simple to understand.

Carnivores need to clean themselves routinely. A kill can be messy, but because there is seldom competition

Total relaxation
In the security of our homes, a cat does not need to find shelter for sleeping. If it is not eating or participating in activity, it contentedly sleeps, typically for more than 18 hours a day.

Interpreting cat language
Cats share a range of murmurs, such as purring and chirping, and high-intensity sounds, such as shrieks and hisses. Kittens use demanding vowel sounds, and in owned cats, these meows are perpetuated into adulthood.

to eat the kill, the cat can consume its quarry slowly, deliberately, and neatly. In a similar fashion, cats groom themselves in a ritualized manner, licking their fur and, for parts of the body that they cannot reach with their tongues, by applying saliva to the paw and rubbing it on the area to be cleansed. After grooming, cats routinely sleep. They sleep a lot—on average, more than 18 hours a day.

For millennia, being a cat has meant being self-sufficient, looking after oneself, and disregarding others. Altruism has never, ever been part of a cat's personality. Everything cats do, they do for themselves. Your cat may snuggle up to you when you are in bed and unwell, but it does so because you are warm and comforting, not to take care of you.

Being a cat means communicating your feelings from a distance, through the position of your ears, the look in your eyes, and the sounds you make. Cats are superb at communicating blatant "go away" signals. Their "come hither" signals are more subtle and, as a result, more difficult for us to interpret easily.

While all cats share common traits, each cat manifests those traits in a unique way, based upon its sex, genetic heritage, and early learning. This is why, as kittens develop, even among those of the same sex and from the same litter, different personalities emerge. Every cat has a unique identity.

Efficient cleaners
Cleanliness is important for the health and vitality of the skin and coat. The cat's barbed tongue is perfect for ridding the hair of mats or debris. Self-grooming in some long-haired cats can lead to swallowed hairballs.

Natural circus performers
Walking a tightrope may be virtually impossible for us, but because of the cat's rapid-responding organs of balance in its ears, this vital ability is fully developed by 12 weeks of age.

Eating habits

CATS ARE OPPORTUNIST hunters. In the wild they survive by eating whenever they catch or find a meal. Their feeding habits in our homes, however, are quite different. Typically, a pet cat will choose to eat between 10 and 20 small meals a day and will continue to feed throughout the day and night. Your pet cat also has a more varied diet than his self-sustaining relatives, and although dry food is not a natural part of the hunter's diet, many domestic cats actively prefer prepared crunchy food.

Fat cats

Cats get fat only if the number of calories they consume is greater than the number of calories they use up in energy. Feral cats are seldom fat, but owned cats often are, especially those that are housebound. Vets estimate that more than one-third of the cats they see are overweight or clinically obese. Neutering increases the predisposition to obesity, so neutered cats should have their food consumption reduced by 10–20 percent.

Eating in peace
To avoid competing with her young kittens, the mother eats separately, removing her food from the bowl. When given a large lump of food, she will slice it into smaller pieces, which she consumes individually.

Comfort and safety
Settling down to eat, this cat adopts a hunched position, with feet drawn back for comfort. The tail is wrapped around the body to prevent it from being stepped on, allowing the cat to concentrate on eating.

"What on earth is this stuff?"

Head tilts to drop unwanted pieces of food

Large canine teeth grasp and tear

Dry morsel
Offered dry food for the first time, this cat stands rather apprehensively to investigate the pieces.

Shearing teeth
Using the razor-sharp carnassial, or side, teeth, the cat slices large lumps of food into small pieces before swallowing. The small front incisors are useful for scraping off tiny pieces of meat or fish.

The cat and the cream
Using mobile tongues, the kittens take four or five laps before each swallow. They are fastidious drinkers, seldom spilling a drop.

Smelling and tasting

YOUR CAT HAS TWICE AS MANY scent receptors in her small nose as you do. She sniffs to pick up information about food, the presence of other cats, and potential danger. From smell she can tell whether a tom owns the territory or if a female is in heat. Your cat is drawn to food by smell, rather than taste, and will never taste anything without smelling it first. Her taste buds are sensitive, distinguishing between salt, bitter, and acid tastes, but she has no taste buds that respond to sweet tastes. Cats that crave chocolate either have been unwittingly trained to do so or are the result of our intervention in breeding.

Memorizing scents
Sniffing cat urine in a clump of grass, this cat draws the scent into the "sex scenting" vomeronasal organ in the roof of the mouth. Cells within that organ trap odor molecules, which are converted into electrical signals and transferred to the brain. In this way, scent memories are formed.

Air is sniffed into the vomeronasal organ

"Hey, look at my spiky tongue!"

Backward-pointing barbs are used for grooming and scraping meat off bones

Grooming tool
Your cat's tongue is long, muscular, and flexible. The sandpaper-like hooks are used in grooming. The taste buds, which include receptors sensitive to the taste of water, are located at the tip, sides, and back.

Wide eyes show excitement at catnip

Cat aphrodisiac
Sniffing a catnip toy stimulates your cat by activating her biochemical pathways. The scent is taken up into the vomeronasal organ, and she rolls around showing her pleasure. This is similar to pre- and post-mating behavior. Only half of all adult cats will sniff, lick, or chew catnip.

Giving pills

While veterinary medicine-makers have produced a selection of "palatable" medicines for cats, it is still difficult to mask taste and smell. Cats don't have taste buds for "sweet," which is a common additive to make medicines taste better. There are "palatable" treats in which medicines may be hidden, but it is often necessary to use a pill-administering device to ensure that medicine is taken.

"Piller" is inserted in mouth and pill released

"Smells good, so it's sure to taste good."

"I guess I shouldn't have eaten that."

1 Exploring by smell
Initially attracted to a toad by its movement, this cat explores further by smelling it. Most cats enjoy hunting amphibians and often present them to their owners as gifts. They will eat them only when absolutely necessary.

Sniffing dramatically differs from regular breathing

2 Reacting dramatically
An unpleasant taste will make a cat salivate profusely in an attempt to dispel the taste as quickly as possible. Medicines may provoke this response in your cat.

The cat's voice

YOUR CAT USES HIS VOICE to welcome you home, beg for food, demand attention, call for a mate, complain, threaten, and protest. The mood your cat is in—angry, indignant, anxious, content—is also revealed in the voice. By the time kittens are 12 weeks old, they have mastered the full range of adult cat vocabulary, which we know includes at least 16 different sounds. Cats can probably distinguish many more. Some individuals and some breeds, especially the Siamese, are more vocal than others.

"Feed me. Please. I'm starving here!"

Hissing and spitting
This cat arches her tongue in fear or anger to force out a jet of hot breath. The hiss is used to intimidate, and the feel and smell of it are just as important as the sound.

The demand meow
This hungry cat is meowing plaintively, asking to be fed. The inflection and intonation of the meow can express a range of feelings. However, sometimes it is only from your cat's begging posture that you can tell he is meowing, since he may make a high-pitched meow, which is out of our range of hearing.

"Where are you? I'm lost! Help!"

Motherly purr
Her kittens busy suckling, this content mother purrs rhythmically. Exactly how a cat purrs is not fully understood, but the sound is thought to be transferred from somewhere behind the larynx. Because the voice box is not used, she can chirp at the same time.

Anxiety attack
The young kitten calls in distress. She makes this anxious cry, which is similar to a baby's, when she is hungry, cold, or away from Mother.

Do cats mimic us?

Cat language can be divided into three general sound categories. Murmurs include purring and the gentle chirping used in greeting or to express contentment. A mother cat will chirrup to beckon her kittens. Vowel sounds such as "meow," "mew," "MEE-ow," and "meOW" are made when the cat is demanding, complaining, or bewildered. High-intensity sounds include the growl, angry wail, snarl, shriek of pain or fear, hiss, spit, and the mating cry of the female.

Rumbling growl

This irritated cat growls with discontent. Her protest begins with clamped jaw and a low rumble. She will then start to hiss or spit if she is in pain or trying to intimidate intruders. Although issuing from the voice box, the growl can be made with a closed mouth, since it is not a vowel sound.

Purring in bliss

Sprawled at ease on a cushion, this cat is purring with pleasure. Such murmurs are normally a sign of a contented and secure cat. Paradoxically, a cat that is upset will also purr as a way of reducing his level of distress.

The call of the wild

It is estimated that almost half the world's 400 million cats live self-sufficient lives, hunting, eating, and reproducing with no human intervention. Many live within our communities, and while some of these "feral" individuals join our households, some house cats also willingly return to full independence.

Balance and hearing

YOUR CAT'S UNCANNY ability to land on his feet, maintaining perfect balance, is directly connected to his acute hearing. Deep in the ear is the vestibular apparatus, which is filled with fluid, tiny floating crystals, and millions of sensitive hairs. These instantly orient the cat so he can turn his body into an upright position. Related to this innate sense of balance is the cat's acute hearing—sharper than either a dog's or a human's. Your cat is able to hear tone so distinctly that he can distinguish between the sound of your car engine and that of an identical size and make of car.

Head rotates first

Loosely attached back bones allow 180° rotation

1 Finding bearings
Falling through the air from a height, this cat begins to orient himself. Sent by the vestibular apparatus, the first messages rotate the head.

Hind-leg muscles begin to respond to instruction to rotate

Ears can be rotated individually

2 Twisting
Once the head and ears have rotated into the correct place, the cat is able to assess his position. Twisting at the waist, he rapidly swings the front of his body around to prepare for landing, despite the fact that his hindquarters may still be facing skyward.

Catching sounds
Natural prey is often hidden in long grass. By moving his ears around, the cat is able to locate the noise precisely and funnel it to the eardrum so that he knows where to pounce. More than 20 muscles in each ear give the cat fine control over its movement.

Vestibular apparatus

The organ of balance, the vestibular apparatus, in the cat's inner ear, contains tiny fluid-filled chambers and canals lined with millions of sensitive hairs and microscopic floating crystals. When a cat moves, the delicate hairs detect movement of both the fluid and crystals, and send messages to the brain, which responds with orientation messages to the body. Both infection and chemicals can damage the organ.

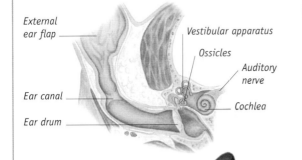

External ear flap

Vestibular apparatus

Ossicles

Auditory nerve

Ear canal

Cochlea

Ear drum

Turning a deaf ear
This blue-eyed white cat suffers from genetic deafness. She does not turn her head in the direction of a sound or move her ears to locate a noise. White cats with one blue and one yellow eye are often deaf only on the blue side.

"And that's a perfect landing."

3 Absorbing shock
Nearing the ground, the front legs stretch out. With no bone attachments to the rest of the body, the forelimbs absorb shock to prevent injury. The body continues to twist as orientation messages are sent to the hindquarters.

Forelimbs stretch out to make ground contact first

4 Landing feet first
Now ready to land on his forepaws, the cat looks confidently ahead at the landing pad. All his muscles are relaxed, because tense muscles are more likely to tear.

Forelimbs act as shock absorbers

Cats' eyes

THE EYES ARE ONE of your cat's most distinctive and mesmerizing features. Appropriately for such opportunist hunters, a cat's eyes are designed to collect the maximum amount of light. The eye's surface, or cornea, is curved, and the lens is very large in comparison to the other dimensions of the eye. In dim light, or when your cat is excited or scared, the pupils dilate; in bright light they can close almost completely, to the slimmest of slits, acting as nature's most practical and efficient sunglasses.

"Do I look like I'm from outer space now?"

Pupils are constricted to thin slits

Shading from glare
With pupils the size of pinpricks, this cat can stare into the sun without damaging his retina. The muscles in the iris allow the pupils to change shape according to the available light. In intense light, the slit pupil closes in the middle, leaving two tiny slits at each end.

Seeing in the dark
In restricted light, this cat's pupils dilate to become almost spherical, allowing as much light as possible to enter the eye. Contrary to popular belief, cats cannot see any better than we can in pitch dark, but their eyes can function in very dim conditions, aiding in dawn and dusk hunting.

Eye care

Head-to-head combat is not uncommon when two cats fight over territory, and their prominent eyes are particularly susceptible to damage. While bacterial infection (conjunctivitis) is common after cat fights, scratch or puncture injury to the cornea is less common. The third eyelid often takes the brunt of fight damage. Transmissible viral and bacterial eye infections are more usual causes of eye damage. Both can cause dangerous wounds to the corneas. Vaccines are available to prevent these transmissible infections.

What your cat sees

Cats see green and blue but not red. This is not a significant weakness, since smell and taste, rather than color, distinguish prey. Cats focus on the middle of the picture, with the periphery remaining slightly cloudy. The images on the right demonstrate the differences between what we see and what your cat sees. He can focus on fast-moving objects clearly because, with his superb flexibility, his head stays level as he bounds along.

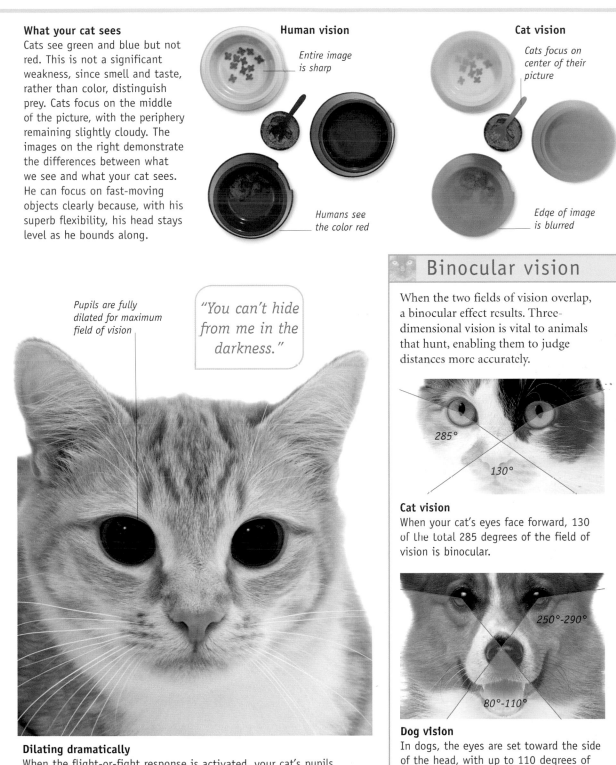

Human vision

Entire image is sharp

Humans see the color red

Cat vision

Cats focus on center of their picture

Edge of image is blurred

Pupils are fully dilated for maximum field of vision

"You can't hide from me in the darkness."

Binocular vision

When the two fields of vision overlap, a binocular effect results. Three-dimensional vision is vital to animals that hunt, enabling them to judge distances more accurately.

285°

130°

Cat vision

When your cat's eyes face forward, 130 of the total 285 degrees of the field of vision is binocular.

250°–290°

80°–110°

Dog vision

In dogs, the eyes are set toward the side of the head, with up to 110 degrees of binocular overlap.

Dilating dramatically

When the flight-or-fight response is activated, your cat's pupils dilate. This creates a wider field of vision and actually allows your cat to see more of any potential danger.

Touching

ALL THE TIME, YOUR CAT is using her well-developed sense of touch to gather information about her surroundings. The most sophisticated touch receptors are contained in the whiskers, which, extending beyond the width of her body, help her to move around confidently. From the information picked up by the whiskers, your cat can determine, for example, whether or not she can fit through a narrow gap. Other touch receptors on the body are sensitive to pressure and texture, responding to such things as the sensation of being petted or the type of surface underfoot. All over your cat's body there are receptors that detect heat and cold. Her preference for the warmth of a fireplace or heat register may well have come from the ancestors that originated from North Africa.

Touching noses
This kitten greets another cat she knows by sniffing his nose. The touch receptors on the nose are already developed at birth and help the kitten find her mother.

"Hello. And how are you today?"

Flattened ears show apprehension at meeting

"Ah, yes, this really is very relaxing."

Measuring spaces

Using muzzle whiskers, this cat is able to gauge whether or not she can squeeze her lithe body through the narrow gap in the fence. As her head comes through, she will direct her whiskers to feel the surface below.

Basking in comfort

As a kitten, this cat enjoys the security and warmth of the girl's lap. However, when he is older, he may not remain in this position or allow her to tickle his tummy, because he may feel far too exposed.

Cat is perfectly content next to radiator

Seeking out heat

Cats love heat and can withstand much higher temperatures than we can. We start to feel uncomfortable if our skin temperature exceeds 112°F (44°C), but your cat will be fine until her skin temperature reaches 126°F (52°C).

Whiskers

Every whisker, or vibrissa, over your cat's eyes, on her elbows, and on her muzzle is rooted in a rich supply of nerve endings. As these specialized antenna-like hairs brush past objects, messages are sent to the brain through nerves that join the optic nerves from the eyes. Even air currents can be felt by the vibrissae, and at night the whiskers help pick out a clear, safe path. If she loses her whiskers, she may bump into objects in the dark, but new whiskers will grow in their place.

Grooming

GROOMING IS NOT only a matter of personal hygiene, it is a reflex behavior. Just as you sometimes scratch your head in thought, your cat may have the urge to groom. Usually your cat will groom herself when she is feeling relaxed, but she may preen if she is frightened. Grooming helps keep the fur in pristine condition and, as the saliva evaporates, can also help your cat regulate her temperature. Your cat is naturally clean. She will instinctively use a specific site as a toilet, and just as fastidiously groom her fur. The licks stimulate glands in the skin to produce an oily film that waterproofs her coat. Her hook-covered tongue removes loose hairs and mats, and she uses her teeth to gnaw at other debris. Long-haired cats may need extra help with grooming. The fine hairs tangle easily and knots often form in the coat.

Leg is raised out of the way to aid grooming

Total cleansing process
This cat sticks her leg up in the air and then reaches around to clean herself. As she removes matted or soiled fur, the grooming action stimulates the scent-producing anal and perianal glands.

Tail and other hind leg are kept flat for balance

"Thank you. I just couldn't reach there."

Mutual grooming
This kitten licks her mother behind the ears and provides a practical solution to an anatomical problem. The mother is totally relaxed. Mutual grooming also strengthens the intimate bond between mother and offspring.

Abrasive tongue combs fur

Clean from top to tail

With her mobile spine, this cat can reach to groom most parts of her body with her tongue. Turning her head almost 180 degrees, she nibbles away at grit and flakes of dead skin on her back. The order in which she washes is random.

"Keeping clean makes me feel good."

1 Washing routine
When your cat grooms herself after being handled, she may be tasting your scent or, more likely, simply masking your scent with her own. Her washing routine is always the same. Saliva is applied to the inside of the forepaw, which is rubbed from back to front in circles on the side of her face.

2 Washing behind the ears
Completing the end of a large washing circle, she brings her paw over her ear. Applying saliva for a final rinse, she will pull her paw over her eyes to complete the washing cycle. Your cat enjoys being stroked on the head because she cannot reach it with her tongue.

Keeping clean and tidy
Cats are immaculate self-cleaners, an attribute that is necessary for a species that kills to eat, but also one that we admire and treasure in an animal with which we share our homes. Each day a typical cat loses as much liquid through saliva used for grooming as it does through passing urine.

Catnapping

YOUR CAT SPENDS more than 18 hours a day sleeping, which is twice as long as most other mammals. Exactly why they spend so much time snoozing is not yet understood. They seem to prefer to take their catnaps during the day and are usually active in the early morning and late evening, when hunting is most productive. When your cat becomes drowsy, she enters a stage of light sleep from which she is easily aroused. Between ten and thirty minutes later, her whole body becomes slack, her position shifts, and she enters a period of deep sleep. On wakening, cats habitually go through a ritual that includes yawning, stretching, and grooming.

Do cats dream?

Sleeping is not a passive state. During deep sleep your cat may flex her paws and twitch her whiskers. She almost certainly dreams, and judging from the amount of electrical activity in the brain, her mind is as active as when she is awake. Also, REM sleep is similar in cats to human REM sleep. After around seven minutes of deep sleep, she returns to a light sleep. The cycle is then repeated.

Snoozing in comfort

These young kittens snooze together, enjoying each other's warmth and the security of the basket. As they get older, they will tend to sleep alone but will still choose warm, secure spots such as closets or your bed for catnaps.

Yawning

Awakening gently, a cat will give a wide yawn to stretch his jaw muscles. Yawning is a sign of nervousness in other species, but this does not appear to be the case with cats.

Tail goes up as she arches her back

Flexing the back

Having woken up slowly, this cat puts her paws together and straightens her hind legs. The elegant arch of her back exercises the muscles. She must keep her finely honed body in peak condition so that she is always ready to produce the short bursts of energy that a hunter requires.

Flexible spine extends fully

"There's nothing like a good stretch."

"Mmm, nice. That hits the spot."

Claws are extended in the stretch

Stretching

After arching her back one way, the cat reaches forward to stretch the muscles in her front legs, claws, and neck. Circulation to her extremities is revived and her sense of touch is reawakened.

Waking scratch

At the finale of the stretching ritual, the kitten grooms herself—a habit that is similar to our morning routine.

Toms and queens

THERE ARE SEVERAL subtle behavioral differences between male and female cats. Unneutered males are usually more destructive and more active than females, while females are generally more playful and friendly—more inclined to be affectionate and more hygienic than their male counterparts.

Male cats roam over large territories, marking them out frequently with their pungent urine. They fight for possession of the territory and for the right to mate with the females within it. Neutering can help diminish a male cat's need to roam, spray, and fight, although it does not always affect all these behaviors to the same extent. Males that are neutered before they reach puberty do not develop secondary sex characteristics, but if they are neutered after puberty, all the physical secondary sex characteristics are retained.

"I'm delicate because I'm a lady."

Tomcat
Secondary sex characteristics—such as prominent cheek ruffs and thick neck skin—have developed in this tomcat because it has not been neutered. Likewise, if a lion is neutered before puberty, he will not develop a mane.

Entire female
This female has a typically delicate face and bone structure. Her slight body is also considerably smaller than a male cat's. In some breeds, females grow to only 60 percent of the size of their male counterparts.

Neutered female

The effect neutering has on behavior is far less dramatic in females than in males. Entire males and females have significantly different behavior repertoires from each other, but once neutered they both tend to behave more like the unneutered female than the unneutered male. Neutering reduces the need to roam, so all neutered cats are more likely to stay nearer to the home territory of your yard.

Thick-skinned toms

Some cats might fight over hunting territory, but, as with most mammals, tomcats also fight head to head for possession of breeding territory. Resultant injuries are most likely to occur to the face and neck, and nature has responded to this by thickening the cheek skin—giving the tomcat its distinctively "jowly" appearance—and also by thickening the skin over the neck. Indeed, the skin over the neck can become so thick that it can be difficult to penetrate, and routine injections sometimes need to be given in a different location.

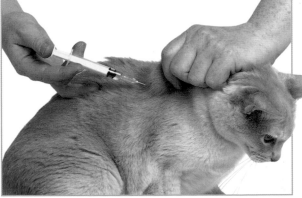

Neutered male

The excitability and destructiveness of male cats does not seem to change with neutering. If males develop unpleasant sex-related behaviors, neutering later is just as effective in correcting the problem as neutering in advance.

Interpreting personality

ALTHOUGH ALL CATS share some behavior
patterns with all other cats, each individual has its
own personality. Some are friendly, assertive, and
bold; others are nervous, timid, and shy. Personality
is partly genetic, inherited from the family, although
we have not yet created inherited temperament
differences as great as we have between breeds of dogs.
Early experience at kitten stage is also very important
in creating personalities. Kittens that are petted
and played with are more likely to develop into
confident cats. Definitions applied to human
personalities can also be used to describe your cat.
The extrovert or outgoing cat is sociable, lively,
assertive, and adventurous; the neurotic or reserved
type is shy, moody, emotional, tense, and anxious.

*"Look out!
Flying cat
attack!"*

*"Is it okay
if I just hold
on to you?"*

*Physical contact
is important in
social activity*

Playful personality
Kittens cuddle and jostle with one another, often touching
heads, as part of their normal social development. If they
grow up without playing with other kittens, they do not
develop a complete repertoire of cat behavior.

Outgoing individual
Playful batting and teasing is common between lively
kittens. This sort of extrovert behavior during kittenhood
often leads to similar behavior later in life, but it is not
always possible to predict a cat's future personality.

"Too slow, brother. You missed me."

Breeds and colors

Some breeds of cats, especially newer breeds such as the Ragdoll, are promoted for laid-back temperaments. This has yet to be thoroughly investigated, but surveys indicate that Foreign or Oriental breeds are noisier and more gregarious, while long-haired cats are more self-contained than average cats. In foxes and dogs, there are reported differences in personality and behavior between golden, and silver or black-colored populations, but as yet there are no studies to show coat-color-related differences in cat personalities.

Facial expression shows worry

Apprehensive adult
An introvert personality usually develops when the kitten lacks social contact. Although slow, quiet, and less responsive than an extrovert, the cautious cat often learns faster and is easier to train.

Timid face shows apprehension

Dominant kitten
Physically dexterous, this extrovert kitten is paw-fighting with her sibling. The outgoing character is accentuated by gregarious play activity. Dominant kittens grow to become dominant cats, since the personality trait is already present in the genes.

Dominant hindquarters stance

Shy puss
Watchful, tense, and solitary, the introvert peeps out from behind an object. Lacking self-confidence and often fearful of, or hostile toward, people and other cats, the introvert cat establishes his character in the first weeks of life.

Reading a cat's face

TO HUMAN EYES the cat's face is often inscrutable, but to other cats the slightest change in expression can mean many things. Cats are not highly sociable, so they have little need for cooperative signals. The position of the ears will usually give you the most accurate clue to your cat's mood. Unlike humans or dogs, cats have not developed a facial expression or gesture—such as a friendly wave or a tail-wag—that is universally recognized as a greeting. A cat's face simply maintains a relaxed and alert look, even when he is truly pleased to see you. On the other hand, the cat's face is exquisitely expressive at telling you "goodbye." Ears, eyes, whiskers, and mouth leave you in no doubt as to the intended message.

The ears and eyes have it

The cat is superbly equipped to use its ears to send out the equivalent of semaphore signals. There are more than 20 muscles that control the position of the ears. When a cat is relaxed, greeting, or exploring, the ears are held forward. Ears down indicate aggression; ears pinned back signal either fear or aggression, or both. Some cats, such as the Maine coon, have extra ear tufts that accentuate ear position. A cat's eyes are relatively larger than the eyes of other domesticated species, and they can also be used to reveal the individual's mood. When your cat is completely relaxed, the eyes will shut. If frightened, the "fight-or-flight" response is automatically activated, and secreted adrenalin causes the pupils to dilate.

The contented cat
Cats reveal their pleasure by half-closing their eyes in a reverie of contentment. This expression, with ears forward, is often accompanied by purring and is the ultimate sign of relaxation. The cat is free from any fear or worry.

The relaxed and alert cat
This is the most common facial expression. It gives no "go-away" signal and is used when cats greet us, when they demand attention, lie down, sit, stand, walk, or trot. It communicates no danger to other cats.

Ears are back slightly

Pupils remain constricted

The ambivalent cat
Twitching ears mean your cat is uncertain of how she feels. Her mood can develop in any direction.

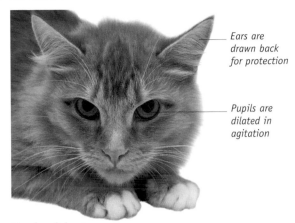

Ears are drawn back for protection

Pupils are dilated in agitation

The fearful cat
When your cat is afraid, her ears fold down. In extreme fear, her ears will flatten completely.

Ear position is upright and alert

Scent receptor is positioned above roof of mouth

The flehmening cat
The flehmen, a sneering expression, occurs when a male picks up the scent of urine of a female in heat.

Ears move forward to pick up noises

Dilated pupils indicate excitement

The curious cat
The inquisitive cat pricks his ears forward to funnel in sounds. The pupils are slightly dilated.

Erect, furled-back ears show anger

Swept-forward whiskers indicate bad temper

The angry cat
When a dominantly aggressive cat gets annoyed, the pupils remain constricted.

Dilated pupils signal fearful aggression

Teeth bared as fierce weapons

The aggressive cat
The pupils are dilated in fear. The cat opens her mouth wide to hiss, spit, and show sharp teeth.

Feline faces
Look into the eyes of any cat, and it's instantly apparent that cats think, ponder, and determine before they act or react. They may all share the same range of emotions, may all have the same array of potentials, but each is a unique individual with a distinctive personality.

5 LIVING WITH US

If your cat could talk, would you be pleased with what you hear? "Do this!", "Do that!", "Pay attention to me. I'm the boss in this household!" While most of us acknowledge that our cats may live with us in our homes, that in law they may be our property, our chattels, we also know that we really don't "own" cats. Cats live with us because they selfishly know it's in their own interests. By good fortune, the benefits are mutual. Just as we provide cats with safety, security, comfort, and nourishment, they provide us with immutability, constancy, intimacy, and an ever-present reminder of just how beautiful nature can be.

When living with a cat, one of the most difficult decisions is whether or not to let it venture outdoors. The outdoor cat is free to act out its natural behaviors, to hunt, to patrol. But it is also exposed to dramatic risk and has, at least statistically, a greatly reduced life expectancy. You may not be a pack leader to your cat as you are to a dog, but you are still the household decision-maker, responsible for ensuring that the outdoor cat is as safe as possible and that the indoor cat has his energies channeled and controlled. It is surprisingly easy to train your cat to come on command and to play with you on your terms rather than his. It is just as easy to train him to use a litter box indoors or a sandbox outdoors, and to negotiate a cat door between his indoor and outdoor worlds.

Early handling
Kittens that are liberally handled between the ages of three and seven weeks of age grow up to be content to live in our homes. They also learn faster than kittens that were not "socialized" during that formative period.

Natural playfulness
Through selective breeding and early learning, adult cats are lifelong kittens, often happy to play. Some toys are designed for cats to play with on their own, while others are interactive, designed for you to enjoy with your cat.

The initial meetings with other family members—and that includes other cats and dogs—should be carefully planned so that the encounters are not just safe but also as pleasant as possible for both parties. It's up to us to ensure that cats live in our world as harmoniously as possible. That harmony can be broken when we misunderstand, as we commonly do, why cats do what cats do. Their use of urine, feces, and visible scratching posts to mark their territory is brilliantly adaptive from an evolutionary perspective, but such activities can also be seriously annoying to many cat owners. Fortunately, with a little sensitive help from us, these natural feline behaviors can be channeled in directions that we find aesthetically acceptable.

From my perspective as a practicing vet, probably the most frustrating characteristic of cats is their natural inclination to hide any indications that they are unwell. It is up to you, as the cat's guardian, to be perceptive about your cat's behavior, to read the sometimes very subtle signs of illness, and to seek medical attention for him or her when it is needed. Living with a very elderly, dignified cat can be just like living with a person with Alzheimer's disease, but even in these sometimes-trying circumstances, our own need to feel wanted is satisfied by the rewards we get from our cats choosing to live alongside us in our homes.

Indoors or outdoors?
If your home has access to the outdoors, this is a difficult decision. Outdoor cats have an outlet for hunting, patrolling, territory-marking, and even fighting, but the risks can be enormous.

The extended family
Dogs naturally chase cats, and there are potential dangers when the two species live together. These risks are reduced when puppies meet cats and are initially intimidated by a hiss, spit, growl, or swipe of a paw. Always plan and control first meetings.

The arrival

WHILE SOME CATS are able to settle into new homes almost immediately, others take time to adjust to their new surroundings. Prepare your house and family in advance, and start off on the right foot. Make sure your cat is healthy, and give her a safe personal space and time to explore her new environment. When you get your cat home, open the door to the car carrier and allow her to wander around in her own time. Leaving a bowl of food or a few cat treats lying around will help break the ice. As soon as you can, put your cat's collar and ID tag on, just in case someone leaves the door open and she bolts. Give her a short, distinctive-sounding name, and use the name every time you call her.

"This necklace will help if I get lost."

"Now this is what I call comfort."

Sleeping space

Where your cat sleeps is up to you, but her natural inclination is based on age and previous experience. Despite your providing them with comfortable bedding, kittens may prefer to sleep with you, while older, independent cats will probably seek out a comfy space of their own.

ID collars

The most visible means of identification is an engraved tag with your phone number on it; this is also a good, immediate way to help ensure your cat's safe return. More reliable, however, is a microchip the size of a grain of rice implanted under the neck skin.

Climbing

It was not until the late 1990s, when Canadian researchers studying the cat's middle ear discovered that it was built not just for a fixed axis of rotation but also to accommodate for three-dimensional motion, that there was an anatomical explanation for why cats have such good three-dimensional balance— and more pragmatically, why cats climb curtains! Regardless of its size, your new arrival will have the ability, and probably the inclination, to climb. Initially it will use its claws, crampon-style, to climb your legs as well as the curtains. If you don't want your curtains climbed, redirect this activity by providing your cat with its own climbing frame.

Eating habits

Moving is a stressful experience for cats, so you should continue feeding them whatever they have been eating previously, at least for a few days, before making any changes to their diet. Always feed your cat in the same location and at the same time of day.

"Where am I now? Where's all my stuff?"

Getting acclimatized

Any new cat needs time to adjust to its new surroundings. Remind children not to be too noisy or excitable with the new arrival. Allow the cat to investigate the single room in which you will initially keep her. Let her discover the litter box, in one corner of the room, and food and water, which should be well away from the litter box. Leave a few toys lying around to encourage her to play. Show your cat where her scratching post is, too; the post is a territory marker and should be placed near the cat's sleeping area.

Your best friend

THE SATISFACTION WE DERIVE from caring for living things is at the root of our survival as a species. It is also the reason why so many of us find such pleasure in sharing our homes with cats. Curiously, cats may be even better than children in fulfilling our need to nurture: they never grow up and are always dependent on us. Stroking them indulges our desire for closeness. Talking, touching, and eye-to-eye contact create an intimacy that is sometimes easier to maintain with a cat than with another person. Cats provide us with a reassuring constancy in our lives, which we like to interpret as loyalty.

"I like to be tickled under my chin."

"That's an interesting head smell."

Secure footing
The kittens feel most secure on the ground and are happy to be petted. Stroking the chin satisfies the kitten's need to leave her scent.

Kitten struggles to move because he feels insecure

Learning to socialize
Kittens are "socialized" when they are handled and played with. The child also learns that there is a limit to the length of time that they enjoy being handled.

Changed by domestication

The domestic cat looks almost identical to its North African wild cat ancestor, but underneath the similar exteriors there are certain significant differences. Wild cats don't like being touched, even by each other, while domestic cats thrive on physical intimacy. The most dramatic difference, though, is the reduction in the size of the domestic cat's brain, which is fully one-third smaller than that of its ancestor. This does not mean a reduction in thinking ability; in fact, what it indicates is that the brain capacity formerly required for certain tasks is no longer necessary. Such tasks include mapping territory, tracking prey, and finding their own way back home.

Cat is relaxed and trusts in her companion

Lap of luxury
Lying on your warm lap, your cat will lower its state of arousal. She kneads your leg with her claws, which is a comfort behavior, and shows her appreciation by arching her neck back to try to give you a friendly "head rub."

Intimate relationship
Stroking your cat is very relaxing. Lying on your chest, enjoying the caresses, he makes a perfect listener. He sees you as a mother substitute, displaying none of the competitive behavior that normally occurs between two cats.

Mutual satisfaction
Feeling secure, the mother cat licks your hand as she would her own kittens, and you enjoy stroking the fur under her chin. Children also benefit from the affection within a family for a pet cat.

Your cat's best friend

FOR A CAT, humans make good cat substitutes. In many ways, cats enjoy warmer, more convivial relations with us than they do with other felines. Humans are almost ideal social companions because they do not represent any kind of threat. We do not compete for food, territory, or sexual supremacy—factors that interfere in the relationships between cats. When raised in close proximity to us, cats look upon humans as being "feline" enough to be treated as fellow cats, while sufficiently different not to be a danger. A lasting dependency and friendship can develop between a cat and a human being, with the cat regarding its owner as an all-powerful, all-providing mother.

Grooming time
Long-haired breeds may need help to keep their coats in condition and to prevent them from becoming matted. Most cats enjoy grooming because the sensation is similar to that experienced as kittens, when Mom licked their fur.

Nose is activated by smell of food

"Mmmm. Something smells good."

Mealtime
The mother cat reaches up to ask for her food, smelling it curiously. This type of begging action can also be seen in kittens when their mother returns to the litter with a mouse after being away hunting.

Staying healthy
Cats depend in part on humans to help them maintain their health, so visiting the vet is an occasional necessity. Train your cat from an early age to travel in a cat basket. Always grasp your cat firmly when putting her into the basket.

Collecting cats

Psychologists say that "cat collectors," people who devote their lives to homing cats, exhibit "exaggerated caring" behavior. Vets know that indulgence can affect a cat's behavior. Cats with conditions such as "learned helplessness" or "exaggerated attention-seeking" are more likely to be owned by people, often those living alone, who talk to their cats as if they were humans, keep their cats indoors for safety, say their cats are central to their lives, are reluctant to take vacations because they don't want to leave their cats, and spend little time with other people.

The dependent feline
Reaching up, this cat sniffs her owner's hand in greeting. She tries to get as close as possible to give a head rub—the cat's natural way of saying hello. Human interaction has perpetuated the dependency of the kitten on its mother. The result is a domestic cat that actively seeks out human companionship, relying on us for fundamental needs.

Position of hind legs allows for full stretch

Being handled

YOUR CAT IS NOT INSTINCTIVELY GREGARIOUS and can resent incorrect handling. She is graceful, dignified, clean, independent, and sensuous, so it is often impossible to resist touching her. A cat unaccustomed to being picked up will allow it only if she feels relaxed, comfortable, and secure. A cat that was not stroked as a kitten will fiercely resist handling. Kittens should be handled for at least 40 minutes each day from two weeks of age onward. The more handling they receive when they are young, the more they will enjoy future handling. However, constant petting may produce mixed emotions. Cats can reveal their ambivalence by biting your hand and then coming back for more affection. An aggressive response is most likely when you rub the cat's belly, because it is the least protected part of a cat's body, never touched by other cats.

Cat shows pleasure by being rubbed firmly behind the ears

The head rub
By rubbing her head against your hand, the cat leaves her marking scent. Unable to groom behind the ears with her tongue, the cat likes being caressed here. Your strokes are similar to the licks her mother once gave her.

Medicine time
A cat will try to swat or bite you when you give it a pill. Hold the head firmly with one hand and flex it back to open the mouth. Drop the pill in and then shut the mouth. Rub the throat to encourage the cat to swallow the pill.

Fleas and ringworm

While human fleas and dogs fleas are uncommon, even rare, the cat flea multiplies in vast numbers wherever there are cats. A dog's fleas are usually cat fleas. So, too, are the fleas that occasionally bite us. When handling cats, especially ones you don't know, or when bringing a new cat home, always check for fleas. Also, all cats, but especially long-haired ones, can carry and transmit ringworm without showing clinical signs of the disease.

1 Supporting hands
Pick the cat up with one hand on its chest behind the forepaws and the other under the hindquarters. This supports the full weight and avoids any discomfort to the legs or rib cage.

2 The handover
The limp tail and hanging paws show that the cat is relaxed as it is handed over to the girl. The child must have the cat firmly in both hands before you release your hold.

3 Sitting comfortably
For a cat, being cradled is unnatural and unfamiliar. Preferring to be upright, the cat will tolerate being held like this only if it feels completely secure and relaxed with the girl.

Correct handling
Support the kitten's hindquarters with the palm of one hand while cradling the forelimbs and head with the other. Never pick up a kitten by the scruff of the neck as its mother does, because this can damage her fragile body. A kitten must be handled frequently to ensure that she enjoys being petted later in life.

"Hold me right and I'll relax."

Correct support enables kitten to relax

Roaming free

ALTHOUGH YOUR CAT is among the world's most prolific sleepers, he also needs frequent activity. One of his favorite natural pastimes is to make rounds of his territory. He will instinctively practice his hunting skills and leave marks to stake out his domain. If he is denied access to the outdoors, he may spend hours at the window watching the world go by. When he sees something that excites or distresses him, he might back up to the furniture and raise his tail and quiver. Spraying urine inside your home is how he demonstrates his frustration when he is cooped up. This common behavioral problem almost always occurs when access to the outside is limited, or if there are too many cats sharing your home.

Tracking and homing

German and American studies in the 1970s suggested that cats have a "homing sense"—an ability to head in the right direction home if they are less than two-thirds of a mile away—but science now helps us find those who can't find their way home. Identification microchips the size of large rice grains are injected under the skin; these reveal the cat owner's details when read by a scanner. Some microchips contain thermometers, making temperature-taking easier for both the cat and the vet. Thanks to miniaturization, GPS tracking-device receivers attached to collars can locate a cat to within just a few yards.

Tail maintains balance

Walking purposefully
Striding along the garden wall, your cat patrols his territory. He often chooses to adopt human boundaries, such as garden walls or fences, as his own. Unless the weather puts him off, your cat will make daily patrols, leaving his territorial scents. This keeps him trim, exercises his sense of balance, and stimulates his mind.

Pricked ears indicate curiosity

"Nice of them to give me my own door."

Sensitive whiskers gauge width

Venturing outdoors
Your cat is most active at dawn and dusk. He will frequently want to go out early in the morning while you are still asleep. A cat door gives him independence, though initially you may need to help him learn to use it. Try tempting him through with morsels of food at first. However, it is wise to be wary of neighborhood cats following your pet back into your home and staking it out as theirs.

"Just making sure all is as it should be."

Leg stretches out confidently

Living indoors
This indoor cat concentrates on the outside world through the window. If he spots a bird, he may chatter his teeth and swish his tail. He could become agitated if his natural activity is restricted too much.

The big, wide world

There is no doubt that an outdoor life is more stimulating than remaining housebound. On the other hand, there are dangers to consider. Each situation is unique. Before letting your cat venture outdoors, analyze the risks. If they are too great, make sure you create activities for your indoor cat.

Being sociable

YOUR CAT CAN GET ALONG with a wide variety of other animals, as well as those of her own species. Provided a young kitten is introduced between two and seven weeks old, a lasting friendship with another cat or a different species can be established successfully. We always tend to think of the stereotype of dog chasing cat, but in reality many dogs are intimidated by cats. Make sure the first few meetings between a young kitten and potential soulmate are sensitively handled, taking care not to trespass on an existing pet's territory, and the kitten will enjoy the companionship later in life. The resulting friendship is a unique behavioral feature of domestic rather than feral cats.

Territory problems

Initially, a resident pet may not want to share its territory with a new kitten. To make the introduction as smooth as possible, let the resident dog or cat sniff the sleeping newcomer. If your kitten is coming from a breeder, make sure it has already experienced social contact with other species. After seven weeks of age, the kitten can no longer make social bonds, so it will be difficult for the cat ever to be friends with other pets. Remember, though, that a kitten that is not scared of your dog may be at risk from strange dogs. When introducing a new dog to a dog-friendly cat, make sure the dog does not consider the cat to be an interloper on its territory, and that the dog is not one that is likely to chase cats instinctively.

"You're like a big shaggy cat, really."

Well-socialized kitten
Not at all inhibited by the dog, this kitten met dogs often when she was young, so her fear of larger animals is reduced. If you want your pets to be friends, let the kitten mix with dogs when between two and seven weeks old.

Agitated expression
shows insecurity

"You're big
and scary. Can
I trust you?"

First encounters
Introduced to a dog for the first time, this kitten is
terrified. Her fur stands on end and she adopts a defensive
stance. Provided that the meeting is not provocative, the
kitten should be less scared at any subsequent encounters.

Intimidating the stranger
This dominant adult cat defends her home from the new
kitten. Hissing and spitting, she is about to swat the
youngster. Nervous, he pulls back, too inexperienced to
know what is happening. His muted response is confused.

Back legs
are ready to
strike out

"We'll make
quick work of
these shoes."

Making friends
These kittens amuse themselves, playing with the yarn and
each other. The period during which kittens can bond is
over quickly, so it is best to acquire several kittens at once
if you plan to become a multiple-cat family.

Playing with humans
These kittens have discovered that humans make good
playmates. Neither kitten is fearful, but the one on his side,
with his tail up, shows early signs of defensive behavior,
grabbing with his forepaws and kicking with his hind legs.

Exercising mind and body

UNLESS YOUR CAT'S ENERGY can be channeled in a positive way, he may become destructive. After all, he never has to worry about where his next meal is coming from, so there is no need for any real hunting or stalking. The frustrated cat that has surplus energy to burn will chew your plants, scratch your furniture, tear your carpets, and climb the curtains. He may even go berserk for several minutes, running back and forth across the room or around the perimeter, doing the "wall of death"—an amusing and dramatic way to release pent-up energy. Some cats tend to suck wool, usually a sign of premature weaning. To prevent such problems, make sure your cat is always mentally stimulated and has plenty of opportunity for exercise.

"It's not quite gourmet, but it'll do."

Wool sucking
If your young kittens suck fabric, or even you, they may have been weaned too soon from their mothers. Siamese may start sucking after they are around six months old, but this is usually a genetically linked behavioral problem.

Gnawing problem
The myth that cats only eat grass when they are unwell is just that. Although they are carnivores, many cats often nibble grass. Inside, this cat tears at a house plant instead. Make sure that none of your plants are poisonous.

Mental-activity toys

Self-operating toys, such as balls, move on their own when played with. Interactive toys, such as feathers dangling from "fishing poles," give both you and your cat the opportunity to play together. Catnip toys trigger rolling and rubbing in many, but not all, cats.

Colored balls

Furry and feathered catnip-infused toys

Fluffy lure

"Fishing poles"

"Hey, that's mine—leave it alone!"

"I'm going to get this thing now."

Scratching posts
Your cat needs to be able to scratch. Very often after waking, a cat has the urge to claw something, just as we like to stretch. Providing a good post will prevent damage to furniture.

"There's nothing like a good scratch."

Moving target
Standing up on his hind legs, with his tail straight out for balance, this cat is inquisitive about the toy. He will investigate it by feeling, sniffing, tasting, and poking. As it swings back and forth, it will provide him with endless hours of amusement.

Training your cat

CONTRARY TO WHAT SOME SAY, cats are certainly trainable. They are always learning, although they do not respond to some of the ways in which we teach dogs to answer to our commands. A cat learns to do something either because he wants to do it or because you make him think he wants to do it. Cats respond to these forms of mild "aversive conditioning."

Noisemakers
A noisemaker is an alternative surprise tactic. It frightens the cat with its clanging sound.

Spray bottle
Cats dislike jets of water. Use a small water spray to squirt your cat if she claws at the carpet or curtains.

Beanbag
Launch a small beanbag near your cat if he attempts, for example, to climb the curtains.

Mothballs
To prevent your cat from digging up the houseplants, spread mothballs, a smell cats hate, on the soil. Make sure the mothballs are kept away from children.

Aluminum foil
If your cat urinates outside the litter box, spread aluminum foil on the area. Cats do not like the feel of it under their feet and will learn to prefer the litter box.

Select nozzle for an intensive jet of water

Punishing routine
When you see your cat misbehaving and the water spray is handy, simply fire the water the moment he claws the plant. Do not shout, since the cat might then associate the punishment with you.

"I wasn't doing anything, I promise."

1 Retaliating first

You may well be absent when your cat decides to misbehave. In this instance, it is necessary to create "traps" that will discipline him instantly. For example, cover the kitchen counter with pots and pans that are bound to be knocked over when he jumps onto it, or set mousetraps under paper around the base of chewable plants.

Make sure mouse trap is covered sufficiently so it does not close on cat's feet

2 Springing the trap

In order to approach the foliage, this cat must step onto the surrounding paper. This provides enough pressure to spring the mousetrap.

Trap causes puper to "explode," but cat is not injured

Cat backs off after being scared by noise

Gentle tap disciplines cat

Correcting directly
If your cat uses you as a scratching post or sucks at your clothes, gently tap him on the nose, but never inflict pain. Admonish your cat in this way only when he has misbehaved directly toward you.

Positive reinforcement

The forms of "aversive conditioning" shown here should always be used in conjunction with "positive reinforcement"—giving treats, talking in a soothing, comforting voice, petting—when your cat redirects his behavior where you want him to—for example, when he uses a scratching post rather than the furniture to groom his claws. Training your cat to come when you call his name is easy once you know what treats he loves and you use these as both the lure and the reward. Adding an attractive noise, such as shaking the treat package to get his attention, makes compliance even more likely.

The importance of play
Cats need both physical and mental stimulation, and simple, inexpensive toys satisfy these. The best toys are those with attractive odors, that make noises, are soft to touch, and can be grabbed, batted, or pounced on. Your involvement in play intensifies your cat's relationship with you.

Caring for your cat

THE DOMESTIC CAT is a highly adaptable African carnivore that has found living with humans to its liking. We may find some of its natural behaviors, such as territory-marking and toilet habits, socially unacceptable, but when offered proper equipment and given correct training, most cats are able to channel their natural habits into more domesticated directions. With a little help from us, they will readily learn to use litter boxes, scratch on special posts, and eat food that we have prepared for them.

Granting freedom
Your cat's natural desire to climb and wander is so powerful that most want to venture outdoors. They can crawl through tight spaces and have no qualms about learning to squeeze through a cat door once it is understood that the door leads outdoors.

Scoop | Liner | Litter   Compressed | Chalk | Fuller's
                                  wood chips   earth

Choosing litter
Line the box with a plastic bag before filling it with litter. For your cat, the most important quality of litter is how it feels underfoot. Your cat may often develop a preference for one texture over another and may be unwilling to switch to a new type of litter.

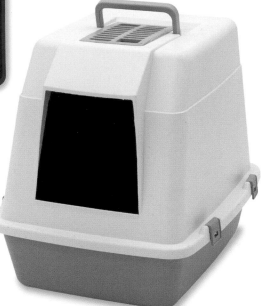

Litter-box training

Cats are naturally hygienic but benefit from a little help from you. To ensure easy litter-box training, stick to the same brand of litter. Generally, cats prefer unscented, fine-grained material. Position the box in an isolated location, away from loud noises, especially those from household appliances. Scoop it daily, and change the litter at least twice weekly. Never discipline your cat by placing her in the litter box. If you have more than one cat and they "ambush" each other in the box, avoid covered litter boxes, so that escape is always possible. Keep one litter box per cat and, ideally, one litter box on each floor of your home.

Creating privacy
Cats are innately litter-box trained, and most prefer the box to be in a quiet, private area. Covered litter boxes meet your cat's security requirements. Some have built-in odor filters.

Moist
canned
food

Dry, crunchy
morsels

Selecting a diet
Although soft food might seem a more natural option, many cats prefer dry food. The crunchy bones of rodent prey are normal food, and dry, pelleted food might duplicate that. Many cats seem to obtain sufficient water from wet food, but they should always have fresh water readily available.

Traveling baskets
Your cat may learn to associate a basket with a trip to the vet. Using the basket as a warm secluded bed while at home trains your cat to associate the carrier with pleasant experiences, too.

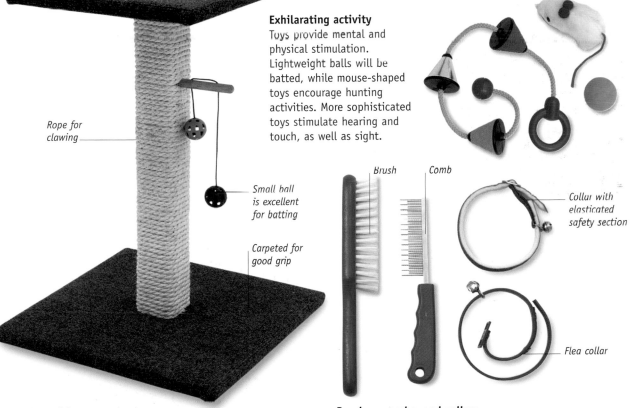

Exhilarating activity
Toys provide mental and physical stimulation. Lightweight balls will be batted, while mouse-shaped toys encourage hunting activities. More sophisticated toys stimulate hearing and touch, as well as sight.

Rope for
clawing

Small ball
is excellent
for batting

Carpeted for
good grip

Brush   Comb

Collar with
elasticated
safety section

Flea collar

Scratching posts
Your cat scratches to leave visible marks on his territory as well as to sharpen his claws. Scratching posts should be left in prominent positions and made of materials in which your cat's claws can easily catch.

Brushes, combs, and collars
Domestic cats, particularly longhairs, often need grooming help from you. If your cat's coat gets very dirty, try giving him a wet or dry bath. Your vet can show you how to trim claws. And collars with bells help save bird populations.

Behavioral problems

SCRATCHING FURNITURE, attacking ankles, being aggressive: these are some of the activities that cats find exhilarating but we find annoying. With the right approach, most feline behavior problems can be corrected, but first you should check with your vet to make sure any behavioral change is not caused by a medical problem. Before tackling a behavior problem you must determine whether stress is involved; if it is, you must first find a way to reduce it. This may simply mean buying some climbing and scratching posts or a few toys for kitty to chase and catch to express his natural predatory behavior. If problems persist and you feel stress is a factor, your vet can supply a synthetic facial pheromone treatment that can help pacify cats or contribute toward reducing tension, aimed at both other cats and people.

Ankle ambushing
A cat attacking your ankles can be painful. Although this is a natural play activity, there is sometimes a sexual component involved, even in neutered cats. Male cats tend to ambush ankles more than females do.

"Why can't we all just get along?"

Common causes of stress
The most common stresses that cause behavior problems in cats are those that threaten their "resources"—that is, their territory (specifically your home) and the attention they get from you. A new cat, a new baby, a puppy, or strangers may trigger emotional conflict, which might be demonstrated by increased scratching, urine-spraying, and defecating.

"Don't mess with me—I'm crazy today."

Cat bullies
Aggression is a normal behavior in cats and can be seen in various forms. Pain, of course, triggers aggression. So does getting overexcited when playing too vigorously. Aggression toward other cats or dogs may be seen after a break in relationships—for example, after another cat has been at the vet's or in a kennel.

Can someone help?

Feline behavior problems can be frustrating, even irritating, but they are rarely unique, almost always explainable, and usually correctable. Your veterinary clinic's staff should be able to help with most of your concerns and, in particular, differentiate between what you think is a behavior problem and what may be a medical concern. The website of the nonprofit Cats International provides excellent advice on a wide range of common issues. For more complicated behavior problems, ask your veterinarian or a nearby veterinary teaching hospital to help you locate a qualified animal behaviorist who is skilled at interpreting and correcting behavior concerns.

Love bites

What behaviorists call "petting aggression" is surprisingly common. This is when a cat that is seemingly enjoying your petting suddenly lashes out and bites. Sometimes the grab and bite is inhibited—the cat only mouths you—but equally it may be a full bite. Cats do this because they have mixed emotions. Although they enjoy your contact, which reminds them of their mother licking them, unrelated adult cats only make contact with each other when fighting or mating. With these mixed signals, most cats eventually feel uneasy.

"These mixed signals are killing me!"

Claws remain sheathed in play fight

Cat bites its aggressor in playful manner

Back feet kick in pedaling motion

Behavioral problems continued

Eating houseplants

Make sure none of your houseplants are potentially dangerous if chewed by your cat. Regardless of toxicity, keep plants out of reach—suspended in hanging baskets, for example—and use a commercial deterrent spray on any plant leaves that might fall within your cat's reach.

Claws are groomed or sharpened on furniture

"I love the feel of leather under foot."

Scratching and clawing furniture

As normal for a cat as urinating and defecating, scratching exercises the claws, sharpens the nails, and stretches the muscles. Scratching is also a territorial behavior, leaving visible marks for other cats. You can't eliminate this normal behavior, but it can be redirected. Start by buying scratching posts—vertical or horizontal, depending on your cat's preference. Place them in all the locations your cat likes to scratch, using catnip as an incentive if needed.

"Mmm, tasty—but it could make me sick."

Spraying urine

A cat marks its home territory by spraying urine. While males are more inclined to spray urine, both sexes do so—some even after they are neutered. It is often triggered by stress. Until you are able to identify the cause of the spraying, when you leave your cat alone at home, try keeping him in a large pen, with enough room for a litter box, blanket, and food and water bowls.

Double therapy

Correcting behavioral problems often involves a dual approach—both "attraction" and "aversion." Attraction is self-explanatory. Cats have a variety of natural needs, many of them involving marking their territory with urine, feces, and scratch marks. Ensure that there are attractive locations in your home and yard for these activities. To prevent your cat from digging in your flower bed, provide a small isolated sandbox for your cat to use. Aversion therapy discourages your cat from locations or behaviors (*see pp.140–41*). If aversion therapy such as a squirt of water is carried out by you, make sure your cat does not associate you with the mild aversive experience. Aversion therapies such as double-sided tape or infrared noisemakers can be used in your absence.

Jumping on counters

Cats like to survey their manors from a good height. Kitchen counters and tables are also ideal for hunting for food, so make sure this is not rewarded by not leaving food lying around. Food isn't always the problem: your cat may simply use the area as a high viewing location, so set aside an elevated location especially for this purpose.

Cat enjoys being at elevated height

Signs of ill health

FOR THE HEALTHY CAT, one day is much like the next. Routines and rhythms are invariably maintained. Even the slightest alteration from their routine may be an important indicator of ill health. Cats pretend nothing is wrong, so it is up to you to recognize when help is needed. Early in your relationship with your cat, make sure you accustom it to your routine handling and play. Habituate your cat to your opening its mouth, feeling its abdomen, and looking in its ears. Cats may try to hide signs that they are unwell, but observant owners notice subtle changes—for example, a disinclination to sleep in the usual places, an unwillingness to climb, or a change in eating or drinking routines. Subtle changes may indicate significant concerns.

Changes in gum and lip color
Gum color indicates what is happening to the circulation and how much oxygen there is in the red blood cells. Seek veterinary advice for any gum coloring other than pink. Examine the chin and lips, too. There should be no inflammation, swelling, or unpleasant odor. Disregard any black pigmented areas.

Chest movements can reveal
respiratory problems

"I'm having trouble catching my breath."

Panting often
indicates breathing
difficulties

"I'm really not in the mood for food."

Appetite and thirst changes
A reduced appetite is always a cause for concern, but so is increased eating, which may indicate an overactive thyroid gland or diabetes. Reduced drinking is worrisome, while increased drinking suggests a wide variety of metabolic diseases. Increased appetite and weight loss in older cats may indicate thyroid problems. Increased appetite and thirst with weight loss are symptoms of diabetes.

Breathing changes
Normal breathing is so light and relaxed that it is virtually indiscernible. Breathing difficulties can be caused by chest and upper-respiratory-tract infections, as well as by asthma, which is a serious, even life-threatening, problem. Trauma to the chest or diaphragm will seriously affect breathing. Contact a vet if there is inexplicable panting.

Dehydration

"Tenting" is usually a good way to check a cat's hydration. Scruff the cat's neck skin and release; the longer the skin takes to return, the greater the problem. For elderly or obese cats, check hydration by feeling the gums. Dehydrated individuals have dry, sticky gums. Dehydration can be caused by diarrhea, vomiting, excessive urination, or lack of fluid intake because of nausea.

Hyperactive seniors

The kitten in a cat can survive well into old age, but if an older cat acts more like a kitten than it once did, this can be a cause for concern. Two clinical conditions—sugar diabetes and an overactive thyroid gland—are increasingly common in older cats; both cause weight loss and increased activity. Typically, a diabetic cat eats more, drinks much more, is more active, and loses weight. A cat with an overactive thyroid eats more, usually drinks the same, is more active, and loses weight. These conditions are diagnosed by blood sample and treated with medications.

Lethargy

Despite being considered lazy animals, most cats are active and alert for up to eight hours a day. Increased lassitude, even in couch potatoes, may suggest the development of a medical condition, so see your vet immediately. Where obesity is the cause of lethargy, weight loss usually helps.

Position of legs shows lack of interest in moving closer

Weight loss is often worth investigating

Getting older

AS YOUR CAT AGES, you may notice that his mood changes. Some cats become grumpy and irritable, while others grow more affectionate, seeking out their owner for comfort. Old age can also bring on a change in your cat's appetite—he may develop preferences for certain foods, or demand to be fed more or less frequently. The gradual changes of old age are inevitable, but your elderly pet will give you as much pleasure in his later years as he did as a kitten. You may need to adapt the way you treat your cat when he gets past his prime. For example, try not to disturb him unnecessarily when he is sleeping. Let him decide when he wants to be petted. Reduce the amount of protein in his diet, since he will need less energy and his kidneys are not as efficient. A well-cared-for pet cat should live to 15 or more years.

"I don't feel I'm looking my best."

Putting on weight
This Persian cat has put on a few extra pounds in his old age. His coat has also developed mats because he finds it difficult to groom. It is unusual for a healthy cat to become overweight. Unlike dogs, they are not obsessive about food, although some are unwittingly trained by their owners to be so.

Lack of exercise can lead to weight gain

Matted coat develops as he finds grooming more difficult

Cat and human years

Cats are living longer than ever before, thanks to improved disease prevention, advanced medical care, balanced diets, and increased indoor living. This means that the theory of seven human years equating to one cat year is no longer valid. Here is an alternative way to compare the age of your cat to human equivalents.

Cat age	Human equivalent
1 month	10 months
3 months	7 years
6 months	9 years
1 year	24 years
2 years	36 years
3 years	42 years
4 years	45 years
5 years	48 years

… and so on, in steps of three cat years per human year …

18 years	87 years
19 years	90 years
20 years	93 years

"I've got to take it easier these days."

Eyesight begins to fail

Weight loss is common in older cats

Losing weight
In her advancing years, this cat has grown to be rather thin. Overactivity of the thyroid gland sometimes causes cats to become hyperactive, which can result in dramatic weight loss. So can diabetes, impaired kidney function, and other treatable conditions.

Assessing a cat's character

CAT OWNERS UNDERSTAND that each cat is an individual with its own personality. Defining the individual's uniqueness is difficult. All cats share their behaviors with all other cats, but the varying degrees of these behaviors create temperaments. Each individual is affected by genetics, hormones, the environment in which the cat finds itself, and learning.

This means that some breeds almost certainly have traits that can be described as "breed personality." The Siamese, for example, is more vocal than other breeds. Research with other mammals, such as foxes and rats, has shown that personality is linked to coat color. To date, however, no large surveys have been conducted to find whether personality is associated with breed of cat.

Cat images
Many people associate felines with warmth, sensuousness, softness, and all things maternal and feminine. This is good for cats because we will care for them generously. Sadly, almost one in four people think cats are cunning, spiteful, and deceitful, and so they treat them with disdain.

Shy personality
This long-haired tortoiseshell is more withdrawn and quieter than the average cat. These characteristics may be genetically linked to coat length.

Oriental build
Cats with long, lean bodies are more likely to have gregarious, outgoing personalities than their sturdier cousins. They are also more protective of their home territories and are usually more vocal and demonstrative.

Your cat's personality

Cat owners tend to be particularly good observers. Asking owners about their cat's behavior is one way in which scientists are able to research cat personality. It is possible to assess your own cat by using the questionnaire below. Simply score each group of questions separately, adding up the numbers to help you judge exactly how sociable, alert, and equable your own cat is.

To help in a worldwide study of cat behavior, please photocopy the completed questionnaire and send it to: Dr. Bruce Fogle, Box DK, 86 York Street, London W1H 1QS, England.

Check the most appropriate box from 1 to 5 for each of the statements below.	Almost always (1)	Usually (2)	Variably (3)	Rarely (4)	Almost never (5)	Assess your cat's personality by adding up the scores for each section.
1. My cat:						**1. Sociability**
Tolerates handling						A low score (12 or under) means your cat is highly sociable and well integrated in human society. Cats that have matured before they meet humans are poorly socialized and likely to score high.
Is affectionate						
Demands attention						
Is confident						
Accepts strangers						
2. My cat is:						**2. Alertness**
Excitable						Cats with low scores are the most lively and alert. These felines often have energy to burn and may need organized activity, otherwise they become destructive. A high score (over 15) indicates a reserved or listless pet.
Vocal						
Playful						
Active						
Destructive						
Independent						
3. My cat is:						**3. Equability**
Fearful of familiar cats						Cats that enjoy cat company will score high (over 12) and usually include cats raised permanently from kittenhood with other cats. A low score indicates a cat hater—either too territorial to allow another cat on its turf or too set in its ways to change its attitude.
Hostile to strange cats						
Solitary						
Aggressive						
Tense						

- How old was your cat when you acquired him/her?
- How old is your cat now?
- Is your cat male or female?
- Has your cat been neutered?
- Does your cat have free access to the outdoors?
- In what country do you live?
- What is the breed of your cat?
- What color is your cat?

Index

Useful websites

BREED REGISTRIES
The Cat Fanciers' Association
www.cfainc.org

The Governing Council of the Cat Fancy
www.gccfcats.org

The International Cat Association (TICA)
www.tica.org

Traditional Cat Association, Inc (TCA)
www.traditionalcats.com

GENERAL VETERINARY ASSOCIATIONS
American Veterinary Medical Association
www.avma.org

Association of Veterinarians for
Animal Rights
http://avar.org

Canadian Veterinary Medical Association
http://canadianveterinarians.net

**WELFARE, RESEARCH, AND SPECIAL
INTEREST**
Alley Cat Allies
www.alleycat.org

American Society for the Prevention
of Cruelty to Animals
www.aspca.org

Canadian Society for the Prevention
of Cruelty to Animals
www.spca.com

Cat behavior and resource site
www.messybeast.com

Cats International
www.catsinternational.org

Humane Society of the United States
www.hsus.org

Acknowledgments

Author's acknowledgments

When I wrote *Know Your Cat*, upon which this book is based, I wrote in the acknowledgments, "I didn't know it at the time, and I'm sure that he did not realize it either, but my father, through his collection of animals, primed me from childhood to have an interest in animal behavior. As I write this, he remains a healthy octogenarian, proud as Punch of what his youngest son does. I hope he enjoys showing this book to his friends."

Well, he sure did! Until he gave up driving at the age of 95, he kept a copy of that book in the trunk of his car and showed that acknowledgment to anyone willing (or unwilling) to take a look at it.

This expansion of the original book was possible because those with whom I work created time for me to write. Doctors Veronica Aksmanovic and Grant Petrie and the nursing team—Ashley McManus, Suzi Gray, Angela Bettinson, and Hester Small—are, quite simply, wonderful.

So, too, is the team at Sands Publishing Solutions: David and Sylvia Tombesi-Walton and Simon Murrell. We've worked together before, and I hope we'll continue to do so in the future.

Thanks, too, to Miezan van Zyl, Sarah Larter, and Phil Ormerod at DK, who have ensured that DK's always high standards are maintained.

Publisher's acknowledgments

Dorling Kindersley would like to thank: Natasha Guttmann, Esther Bruml, Karen Tanner, Carolyn Stephenson, Blackie Merrifield, Jenny Berry, Jane Burton, Heather Creasey, Liz Button, Lynn Medcalf, and Margaret Correia for providing cats for photography on location; Steve Gorton and Tim Ridley for location photography.

Packager's acknowledgments

Sands Publishing Solutions would like to thank: Hilary Bird for the index; Debbie Maizels for artworks; and Homie and Rudy for additional feline modeling.

Photographer's acknowledgments

Jane Burton would like to thank: Hazel Taylor, Sue Hall, Di Everett, Les Tolley, and Jane Tedder for help to find, handle, and feed cats; Carolyn Woods for lending cats for photography; Arabella Grinstead and Louisa Hall for modeling.

PICTURE CREDITS

Every attempt has been made to identify and contact copyright holders. The publishers will be glad to rectify, in future editions, any omissions or inaccuracies brought to their attention.
Key: t = top; b = bottom; l = left; r = right; c = center.

All photography by Jane Burton except the following.

For DK:
Paul Bricknell: p.5 br, p.6 bc, p.60 bl, p.122 br, p.124 cr, p.153 tl.
Emma Firth: p.48 bl.
Steve Gorton: p.7 br, p.23 tl, tr, p.24 cl, p.25 r, p.93 bl, p.97 tr, p.98 b, p.115 bl, br, p.119 tl, bl, p.150 tr, p.151 tl.
Frank Greenaway: p.86 bl.
Marc Henrie: p.8 bl, p.10 tr, p.11 br, p.18 cr, p.23 bl, p.61 br, p.130 br.
Jacqui Hurst: p.7 bc.
Colin Keates: p.14 cl.
Dave King: p.4 br, p.10 tl, p.12 bl, br, p.13 bl, p.16 b, p.21 bc, p.24 cr, bl, p.25 bl, p.27 br, p.61 bl, p.63 tr, p.88 bl, p.92 bl, br, p.105 br, p.124 cr, p.150 bl, p.151 cr, b, p.154 tr.
Steve Lyne: p.9 tl, p.65 tl.
Debbie Maizels: p.33 all artworks.
James McConnachie: p.112 tr.
Jane Miller: p.6 br.
Daniel Pangbourne: p.9 br.
Tim Ridley: p.32 cl, p.87 bl, p.115 tr, pp.140–1 all pictures except p.140 br and p.141 bl, p.145 tl.
Kim Taylor: p.102–3 c.
David Ward: p.146 br.
Tim Winter: p.7 bl.
Jerry Young: p.17 tr.

Agencies:
Alamy: Drew Hadley p.21 tr; blickwinkel p.47 tr; Sébastian Baussais p.50–1; Tom Gardner p.51 cr; Junior Bildarchiv p.56 bl; Peter Steiner p.76-77; EPTravelStock p.99 tl; imagebroker p.100–1; Jeff Smith p.120–1; Petra Wegner p.129 cr; Visual&WrittenSL p.142–3.
Corbis: Guenter Rossenbach/zefa p.38–9, Frank Lukasseck/zefa p.66–7, James L. Amos p.81 br, Jonathon Cavendish p.90–1, James L.Amos p.110–1, Richard Hamilton Smith p.134–5.
FLPA: David Hosking p.14 bl; Andrew Parkinson p.16 tr; Angela Hampton p.58 bl, p.79 tr.
Sands Publishing Solutions: Simon Murrell: all background photography; David Tombesi-Walton: p.75 tr, p.104 cr; Sylvia Tombesi-Walton: p.6 bl.